P9-DYD-557

Portrait of Thomas Jefferson at the age of 77 years (1821) by Thomas Sully. Retired from public service, he was at this time involved with the "hobby of my old age," the founding of the University of Virginia.

The Jefferson–Hemings Myth

An American Travesty

PRESENTED BY

The Thomas Jefferson Heritage Society
Charlottesville, Virginia

EDITED BY EYLER ROBERT COATES, SR.

JEFFERSON EDITIONS
CHARLOTTESVILLE, VIRGINIA

COPYRIGHT © 2001 THOMAS JEFFERSON HERITAGE SOCIETY

All rights reserved.
No part of this book may be reproduced or retransmitted in any manner whatsoever,
except in the form of a review, without the written permission of the publisher.
Jefferson Editions
P.O. Box 4482
Charlottesville, VA 22905-4482

LIBRARY OF CONGRESS CATALOGING-IN-PUBLICATION DATA

The Jefferson-Hemings myth: an American travesty / presented by the Thomas Jefferson
Heritage Society; edited by Eyler Robert Coates, Sr.-- 1st ed.
p. cm.
ISBN 0-934211-66-3 (alk. paper)
1. Jefferson, Thomas, 1743-1826--Relations with women. 2. Jefferson, Thomas, 1743-1826--
Relations with slaves. 3. Hemings, Sally. 4. Paternity testing--United States--Case studies.
I. Coates, Eyler Robert.
II. Thomas Jefferson Heritage Society.
E332.2 .J47 2001
973.4'6'092--dc21
2001001468

FIRST EDITION
ISBN 0-934211-66-3

PRINTED AND MANUFACTURED IN THE UNITED STATES OF AMERICA

Jefferson Editions are available at bookstores or directly from the publisher,
or online at http://www.tjheritage.org

"All should be laid open to you without reserve, for there is not a truth existing which I fear, or would wish unknown to the whole world."

Thomas Jefferson to Henry Lee, May 15, 1826
(50 days prior to Thomas Jefferson's death)

TABLE OF CONTENTS

Illustrations

The captions under the illustrations in this book were written by
C. Michael Moffitt, Ph.D.

The photograph of the Houdon bust of Jefferson on the front cover is courtesy of
James McMurry, M.D., and is used by permission.

The photograph of the William Hemings Gravesite on page 36 is courtesy of John
H. Works, Jr., and is printed by permission.

The photograph of the Jefferson Memorial on page 162 is courtesy of
M. Batmanglij, and is printed by permission.

The cover design was by Eyler Robert Coates, Sr.

The quotation on the front cover is from James McClellan, J.D. ,Ph.D., James
Bryce Visiting Fellow in American Studies, Institute of United States Studies,
University of London.

Foreword

The alleged affair between Thomas Jefferson and Sally Hemings began as gossip and was published in 1802 by James Callender during Jefferson's first term as president. In common with the licentious practices in the press of those times, the allegations were widely spread, solely for political purposes, even though these accusations had no foundation in fact. They were promoted back then by Jefferson's enemies, and have been supported more recently by handed-down gossip, distorted scientific conclusions, and false sound-bites, then offered to the public as "revisionist history." Historical revisionism is perfectly legitimate when it rests on a careful reassessment of the past. But what is presented as revision in this case is based on a misleading headline in the journal *Nature*, scientific evidence that was interpreted unscientifically, and conclusions in the media that have no basis in the actual scientific facts.

In early May 2000, a group of concerned businessmen, historians, genealogists, scientists, and patriots formed a corporation called The

Thomas Jefferson Heritage Society, Inc., to undertake an independent and objective review of all the facts and circumstances surrounding the possible paternity of Sally Hemings' children by Thomas Jefferson. This organization was formed as a response by a cross section of citizens to efforts by many historical revisionists to portray Thomas Jefferson as a hypocrite, a liar, and a fraud. In the forefront of this historical revisionist movement is the organization that owns Thomas Jefferson's home, Monticello, the Thomas Jefferson Memorial Foundation (TJMF). A report issued by the TJMF in January 2000 suggested that Thomas Jefferson fathered at least one, and probably all six, of the children of his slave Sally Hemings.

The founders of The Thomas Jefferson Heritage Society believe that the TJMF report is biased—the product of shallow and shoddy scholarship, a selective exclusion of exculpatory evidence, and the exercise of poor judgment on the weight to be given to historical sources, genealogical and scientific evidence, and the legal requirements of paternity, all done in order to achieve an apparently desired conclusion. Admirers of Jefferson had expected a whole lot more from this esteemed body, whose original mission was to perpetuate the reputation of Thomas Jefferson by focusing on his life and accomplishments.

The Thomas Jefferson Heritage Society was formed, therefore, for the purpose of research and scholarship, and to conduct an independent and objective review of the TJMF report and of all the facts and circumstances surrounding the possible paternity of Sally Hemings' children by Thomas Jefferson. The Heritage Society has begun several new research projects on various aspects of this issue which it intends to make available to interested scholars and the general public. This effort, we feel, is of vital importance to the legacy of Thomas Jefferson and to his place in American thought and political philosophy.

In November 1998, the results of DNA testing on descendants of persons related and allegedly related to those involved in the assumed relationship were announced with gross distortions of what the tests actually revealed. When these test results were first released in the British journal *Nature* in late 1998, many in the popular media mischaracterized the results as definitive proof of the fathering of Sally Hemings' children by Thomas Jefferson. The test results themselves, however, tell a different story, especially if one extracts the biased "interpretations" that accompany them and tend to corrupt the results. While the tests did show that one descendant of Sally Hemings had a Jefferson male line haplotype, it has not been scientifically demonstrated that this haplotype extended back through each generation to those male Jeffersons living in 1807, the year in which Sally's last son was conceived. But even if this in fact could be established, there are at least seven Jeffersons other than Thomas with that same haplotype who were frequent visitors to Monticello and may also have been the father.

More important, and generally overlooked in the *Nature* article and the ensuing press reports, were the results of the DNA tests on the "Woodson claim." The rumor of slave children that was started in 1802 by the Callender newspaper articles claimed that Sally Hemings, maid to Jefferson's daughter, had returned from Paris pregnant with a child later born at Monticello and named "Tom," even though no record of the birth exists. About the age of twelve, he supposedly left Monticello and took the name Woodson, and many of his descendants actively promote their claim of a Jefferson ancestry. The DNA tests, however, completely discredited this "Woodson claim." If there was a Tom, he was without doubt not the son of Thomas Jefferson.

After the DNA results were released, the TJMF announced it would conduct a scholarly review of the issues related to the possibility of a Jefferson paternity. But rather than assemble a national panel of historians, genealogists, and other Jefferson specialists as would have been proper for such an important investigation, the TJMF created a "Research Committee" consisting of members selected from its own staff. Their final report, which also omitted a dissenting minority report, was released January 26, 2000. The report concluded that Jefferson not only had fathered Sally's son Eston, but was probably the father of all of Sally Hemings' children. This conclusion was not supported by a new and exhaustive look at the evidence, but rather was no more than the poorly considered opinion of a majority of the committee members who worked at Monticello.

Because of the widespread consternation over the quality of the research demonstrated by the TJMF report, The Thomas Jefferson Heritage Society has initiated several projects to produce a more balanced examination of the possible paternity of Sally Hemings' children by Thomas Jefferson. One of these projects is this book, which seeks to correct the record and examine the evidence with greater insight than has been demonstrated thus far. It also seeks to reveal the machinations that have occurred in the media and in academia which have distorted the evidence and misinformed the public concerning Thomas Jefferson.

Without doubt, Thomas Jefferson is the foremost intellectual founder of our nation, and the chief spokesman for those principles of liberty and self-government that have become the guiding light to oppressed people around the globe. When those people seek the words that express their deepest desires for liberty, they turn almost exclusively to the principles enunciated by Jefferson. The allegations concerning his behavior do not merely provide an interesting sidelight on an otherwise great man. They are, in fact, a frontal assault on him and his principles, and have as a stated purpose by many proponents the aim to throw out those principles and replace them with something new but as yet poorly defined. These accusations have not just been leveled against Thomas Jefferson personally, but they have devolved into a denunciation of everything he stood for, and this we cannot allow to take hold.

Many scholars, including some of those at the TJMF, have adopted the modern "politically correct" propaganda that those who laid the bricks and plowed the fields were the real builders of this nation, not the man who wrote the Declaration of Independence, doubled the size of the nation with the Louisiana Purchase, and established the University of Virginia. These scholars have begun tearing down the reputation of Jefferson and focusing instead more broadly on the lives and the work done by the Negro slaves, and on their contributions to the building of this nation. Their lives and contributions are certainly worthy of recognition. But this should not be done at the expense of the man who, as Willard Sterne Randall wrote, "invented the United States of America." Defending Thomas Jefferson, therefore, has come to mean defending what America means, and we feel compelled to rise to that defense.

This book, then, is offered as part of that defense. And we of The Thomas Jefferson Heritage Society pledge ourselves to continue this struggle in order to shed the light of truth, ever mindful of Jefferson's own words,

> "Truth is great and will prevail if left to herself... She is the proper and sufficient antagonist to error and has nothing to fear from the conflict unless by human interposition disarmed of her natural weapons, free argument and debate; errors ceasing to be dangerous when it is permitted freely to contradict them."

—Thomas Jefferson: Bill for Establishing
Religious Freedom, 1779.

JOHN H. WORKS, JR.
President,
The Thomas Jefferson Heritage Society, Inc.

The Origins of the 'SALLY' Story

Rebecca L. McMurry and James F. McMurry, Jr., M.D.

The most direct statement that can be made about the supposed relationship between Thomas Jefferson and Sally Hemings is this: it is the false, trumped-up story of James Thomson Callender. James Thomson Callender arrived in Philadelphia in 1793 and died in Richmond, Virginia, in 1803.[1] He had fled Great Britain just ahead of the sheriff. He stood accused of authoring or co-authoring a pamphlet entitled the *Political Progress of Britain*. It was deemed seditious by the English government, so they pursued Callender in England and his native Scotland. Callender's ten years in the United States of America were characterized by similar political writings. His style was flamboyant, outrageous, and best compared to modern supermarket tabloids. He was indeed successful in increasing interest in newspapers by spinning facts into fiction and then fictions into fact—all stated with great verbal force. Just as scandal sells today, it pushed up sales of newspapers two centuries ago. Truth was not necessary, only colorful writing. His style applied in America was described by biographer Michael Durey, "This combination of vituperative misanthropy and extreme political values would be a dangerous brew in an environment where political warfare was at a high pitch."[2]

In the course of his ten years in America, Callender managed to slander the first five men who were or became U.S. Presidents: Washington, Adams, Jefferson, Madison, and Monroe. Callender claimed that he had thrown Adams out of the Presidency, though few believed him. His attempts to influence the Congressional elections of 1802 by slanders against Thomas Jefferson, which included the infamous "Sally" story, may have had effects in some places, but Jefferson's party increased its number of seats in Congress.

It is against this background that the "stories" of the alcoholic and misanthropic James T. Callender must be measured. In the September 22, 1802, issue of the Richmond *Recorder*, Callender first stated that he did not know Ferdinando Fairfax, who had returned issues of the *Recorder* with a note that he had not subscribed and did not like it. Callender then went on to speculate at length and in a licentious manner about the character of this man unknown to him.[3]

Callender introduced his attack on the personal character of Thomas Jefferson with his "Sally story" on September 1, 1802. In the following paragraph, Callender capitalized the names "SALLY" and "TOM," to make them stand out.

> It is well known that the man whom it delighteth the people to honor, keeps and for many years has kept his concubine, one of his own slaves. Her name is SALLY. The name of her eldest son is TOM. His features are said to bear a striking although sable resemblance to those of the President himself. The boy is ten or twelve years of age. His mother went to France in the same vessel with Mr. Jefferson and his two daughters.

Callender later retracted the statement that SALLY had accompanied the two daughters to France with Jefferson.[4] He also later retracted a statement that this son of SALLY had gone to France with them, as he was too young.[5]

These charges were answered by Meriwether Jones, editor of the Richmond *Examiner,* on September 25, 1802:

16

When Callender first introduced the name of one of Mr. Jefferson's female servants, I thought that he had casually opened one of his repositories for poison, and that this little lying Viper had sneaked out: but I see I was wrong; that he is nursing the Pet; and that it is his serious wish the story should be credited.

When Mr. Jefferson went to France, he took his eldest daughter with him; the servant that Callender mentioned did not accompany him. Mr. Jefferson left his youngest daughter in the care of Mr. Eppes, a relation, who while he was in France was his Trustee or Agent. This gentleman, always remarkable for his honor and discretion, ordered Sally, when the youngest daughter sailed, to accompany her: he might as well have ordered another; because he had received no direction on that score from his friend. The delicacy of Mr. Eppes, if there had been any foundation for Callender's story, would have forbidden the arrangement.

That this servant woman has a child is very true. But that it is Mr. Jefferson's, or that the connection exists, which Callender mentions, is false.—I call upon him for his evidence. I challenge him to bring it forward.

Despite Jones setting the record straight, Callender and the Federalist press had not tired of the SALLY story. They continued to circulate the story from an edition of one paper to another paper and back into a new edition of the first. In November 1802, Callender bragged from the pages of the *Recorder* that his stories had ended Thomas Jefferson's political career and that it would be impossible for him to be re-elected in 1804. He admitted that he could not have done it alone with only his one newspaper, but the stories had been "quoted by both parties":

> We shall not have done with these fine stories for six months to come . . . we have done more harm to the political importance of Mr. Jefferson within the last five months than all the rest of his criticks, collectively, had been able to accomplish in *ten years*. The circulation of a single paper could not, to be sure, have effected this. But our articles have been quoted by both parties.[6]

Callender's raging attack on Thomas Jefferson had complicated roots. First and foremost was Callender's personality. He was a misanthropic man who attacked prominent figures much of his life; he had a talent for capturing the reader's interest and holding it. If his style had not been so different from the plodding of many other newspapers, it is likely that he would never have been noticed. A few other editors/reporters of his day were just as outrageous, but most were not. His writing was so bold and bombastic that the reader is propelled forward, but it could eventually become tiresome.

Callender combined his style with some troubling personality traits, which would probably get him a quick ticket to the psychiatrist with any modern HMO. His periods of brilliance were likely the high points of a manic-depressive illness. When fatigue from this frantic writing and activity occurred, he turned to alcohol to slow down.[7] Unfortunately, his use of alcohol was just as intemperate as the rest of his daily activity. Unable to find moderation, he had weeks of drunkenness that would cost him jobs and cost his family dearly. Callender's education was a fine one, judging from the references to classics and history which were made in his writing. His emotional troubles eventually brought him down.

His bold attacks against the Federalists during the time of Washington and Adams were helpful to the Republican cause. The Alien and Sedition Acts of 1798 provoked unrest. These laws regarding foreigners and gagging the criticism of anything said or written against the President or a member of Congress were invoked during a period of worries about war with France. But the Federalists' passage of these laws and many taxes during John Adams presidency challenged the spirit of liberty, for which the colonists had made their split with Britain. James T. Callender had become a naturalized citizen to avert deportation under these rules. But his two volumes of the *Prospect Before Us*, which contained ridiculous attacks on both Washington and Adams, became grounds for prosecution under the Sedition Act. When Callender was sent to jail in Richmond, Virginia, under that act, he seemed almost happy to be a martyr to the cause of freedom. Callender was finally released from jail and Jefferson had just been elected President, so Callender demanded from James Madison that a good federal job should be his. He specifically demanded to become Postmaster of Richmond, Virginia. Thomas Jefferson considered his term as President a serious trust and he even resisted the appeals of members of his own party to "throw the rascals out" of federal jobs and supplant them with Republicans. Thus, Jefferson not only refused Callender the job as Postmaster, for which Callender was ill-equipped, but he declared Callender's appeals, cloaked in threats of blackmail, must be refused. Jefferson had sent Callender money on several occasions, as had other prominent Republicans. Callender's spells of drinking had resulted in a needy family and Callender made piteous pleas for "loans," beginning in Philadelphia and continuing in Virginia. Further, Jefferson had a weakness for the cause of freedom of the press and Callender's situation in the prosecution for sedition made his "cause" even more appealing. Jefferson sent money and letters of encouragement to the discouraged Callender. Callender later published the letters when he failed to receive the Postmaster's job.[8]

Callender switched sides after losing his bid for a fine patronage job. No clear evidence has come to light that he was really in the employ of the Federalists, though it appeared so. Given his personality, he may have been opposed to any person or group in power. In the spring of 1802, a printer in Richmond entered into a partnership with Callender to take over as editor of the ailing Richmond *Recorder*. Callender now had an easy venue for his writing, and write he did. However, his attacks on the policies of the new administration were not gaining much popular ground and he switched to personal attacks. By September 1802, the attacks became more vicious. They coincided with the time of the Congressional elections.[9]

These attempts by Callender to take political vengeance on Thomas Jefferson did not succeed, and Jefferson's party increased its numbers in those 1802 Congressional elections. In the spring of 1803, Callender received his children from Philadelphia, where they had been living for nearly five years in the home of Thomas Leiper, a merchant and tobacco manufacturer. At this time Callender went on an extended drinking binge and put out no issues of the *Recorder* for many weeks. He then drowned in the James River in July 1803. Meriwether Jones suggested that Callender's drowning in a state of intoxication was a deliberate suicide.[10]

Callender predicted that, "The name of Sally will walk down to posterity alongside of Mr. Jefferson's own name. The name of Agrippina is as distinctly remembered as that of Nero."[11] But this does not make a false charge any more true. It was an insult clearly born of revenge and a political smear.[12] While Federalist politicians and editors continued to use the story for political purposes, hardly anyone in America believed these slanders. Thomas Jefferson's manner was to patiently steer the public back to a steady course with reason and ignore all personal attacks.

Nonetheless, Jefferson took notice of these charges and denied them privately, but he refused to get into Callender's gutter and do personal battle with him or anyone else.[13]

In the absence of belief in Callender's stories, they might have drifted into oblivion. However, the SALLY story had the scandalous twist which seemed to keep it alive, and there is little doubt that the newspaper articles of 1802 were carefully saved by different people for different reasons. Though newsprint of today becomes yellow in a few years and deteriorates, the newsprint of 1802 was made of better quality materials and has lasted into this century in fair shape. The worldwide reprinting of the 1802 articles, which Callender bragged about, made possible the widespread availability of his slanders for many years later.

In 1870, a son of Sally Hemings, Madison Hemings, told a Census taker in Ross County, Ohio, that he was the son of Thomas Jefferson. Several years later in 1873, a series of articles under the title of "Life Among the Lowly" were published by one of the Census takers of that area, Samuel Wetmore, who had become a newspaper publisher. Wetmore wrote the stories of many African-Americans of the area and the "interview" of Madison Hemings was his premiere piece. In that story published in the *Pike County Republican* (Ohio) of March 1873, the SALLY story was renewed. Madison Hemings related a complicated series of "facts" which he described "as it came down to me." There need be no suggestion of malignant intent on the part of Madison Hemings. These statements were most likely a synthesis of bits and pieces of disparate information about his ancestors, which had been put together as the best recollection of his "family story." However, the facts of the story can be researched today in old documents and other sources, which were unavailable to Madison Hemings.

When Madison Hemings describes his grandmother as the daughter of a sea captain who sailed into the port of Williamsburg, Virginia, he also describes her as the property of "John Wales, a Welchman."[14] This would explain the light skin of the Hemingses, including Sally Hemings.[15] However, in fact, his grandmother was the property of John Wayles's first wife, from her brother, and may have been "leased out" rather than working at the Wayles house in Virginia.[16] John Wayles was English, not Welsh, and Williamsburg was not a port. But there readily could have been talk of sea captains and a ship called the *Williamsburg(h)* at Monticello. Thomas Jefferson's maternal grandfather, Isham Randolph, was a sea captain in his younger years and had a ship called the *Williamsburg(h)*.[17] Thomas Jefferson's uncle Thomas died aboard that ship.[18] Thus, bits and pieces of fact and rumor were pulled together to form Madison Hemings' story "as it came down to me."

The *Pike County Republican* tale of Madison Hemings was rediscovered and became the basis for a 1974 book, *Thomas Jefferson, An Intimate History,* by Fawn M. Brodie. Using this 1873 story, Brodie wove a tale of psychological interpretation based upon selected letters written by Thomas Jefferson. Though the book received poor reviews from historians for its odd psychological ruminations, its allegations of "deceit" and "hypocrisy" of a founding father of the nation made it interesting and even a bestseller.[19]

Popular interest is obviously not a test of truth. Neither the story of Madison Hemings nor the interpretations of the life of Thomas Jefferson by Fawn Brodie contain enough facts to sustain their ideas of a romance between Thomas Jefferson and his slave, Sally Hemings. Brodie suggested, "One must look for feeling, as well as fact, for nuance and metaphor as well as idea and action."[20] In the absence of any written suggestion that Thomas Jefferson had carried on a 30-year-long affair with Sally Hemings, the notion that old letters were destroyed by Jefferson's surviving family has been suggested.[21] It is remarkable indeed, if the family could remove *every trace* of such "evidence" from the voluminous letters and memorabilia of Thomas Jefferson which became widely dispersed.

The only plausible explanation for the absence of any written suggestion of an affair between Jefferson and Sally Hemings is simple: there was none. But the Callender story of SALLY in 1802 was circulated far and wide and became the basis for often-repeated stories and oral traditions.

Cited Sources

1. Michael Durey: *With the Hammer of Truth—James Thomson Callender and America's Early National Heroes.* Charlottesville: University Press of Virginia, 1990, 51. Jones, Meriwether: Richmond *Examiner,* July 27, 1803.

2. Durey, 49.

3. James T. Callender: Richmond *Recorder,* September 22, 1802.

4. Ibid.

5. James T. Callender: Richmond *Recorder,* November 3, 1802.

6. James T. Callender: Richmond *Recorder,* November 17, 1802.

7. A speculation, based on years of medical practice by the author (Dr. McMurry), studies of the writings of Callender, and the descriptions by Callender's biographers. American Psychiatric Association: *Diagnostic and Statistical Manual of Mental Disorders, 4th Edition,* Washington, DC: American Psychiatric Association, 1994 (revised sixth printing, 1997) 350–358 (code 296.40).

8. Durey, 110–147. Dumas Malone: *Jefferson the President, First Term 1801–1805.* Boston: Little, Brown, 1970, 206–233. Noble E. Cunningham, Jr.: *In Pursuit of Reason, the Life of Thomas Jefferson.* Baton Rouge: Louisiana State University Press, 1987. Charles A. Jellison: "That Scoundrel Callender," *Virginia Magazine of History and Biography* (1959) 67:295–306.

9. Durey, 148–163; Malone, 206–233; Cunningham, 114–116, 222; Jellison.

10. Jones.

11. James T. Callender: Richmond *Recorder,* September 29, 1802.

12. Malone; Jellison.

13. Thomas Jefferson: Letter to Robert Livingston, Ambassador to France, October 10, 1802 (Library of Congress).

14. *Pike County Republican* (Ohio), March 13, 1873.

15. Isaac Jefferson: "Memoirs of a Monticello Slave," as dictated to Charles Campbell (1847) in James A. Bear, Jr., Ed.: *Jefferson at Monticello.* Charlottesville: University Press of Virginia, 1967, 4.

16. Will of Francis Eppes, Henrico County (Va.) Wills and Deeds 1725–1737 (Virginia State Library, Microfilm Reel 74) 612. Tripartite prenuptial agreement of John Wayles, Martha Eppes Epes, and her brother/brother-in-law, Henrico County (Va.) Deed Book 1737–1750, p 132 (Virginia State Library, Microfilm Reel 8). Will of John Wayles, Charles City County (Va.) Records of 1737–1774, p 461 (Virginia State Library, Microfilm Roll 1).

17. Gerald Steffens Cowden, *The Randolphs of Turkey Island: A Prosopography of the First Three Generations, 1650–1806.* Ph.D. Dissertation, College of William and Mary, 1977. Ann Arbor, Mich: University Microfilms, p 355. Elizabeth Donnan: *Documents Illustrative of the History of the Slave Trade to America, Volume IV, The Border Colonies and the Southern Colonies* (Carnegie Institution, Washington, D.C., 1935), reprinted New York: Octagon Books, 1965, 203. (Note: Randolph's ship, the *Williamsburg(h)* of 1712, was followed by another ship, *Williamsburg(h)* built in 1735, and owned by another firm.)

18. Catesby Willis Stewart, Ed.: *Woodford Letter Book, 1723–1737,* Verona, Virginia, 1977, 365. Dumas Malone: *Jefferson the Virginian.* Boston: Little, Brown, 1948, 9.

19. T. Harry Williams: "On the Couch at Monticello," *Reviews in American History* (December 1974), 523–529. Winthrop Jordan: Review, *William and Mary Quarterly,* 3rd Series (1975), 510–511.

20. Fawn M. Brodie: *Thomas Jefferson, An Intimate History.* New York: Norton, 1974 and Bantam Books, 1975, p xii.

21. Tina Andrews: television play, *"Sally Hemings, An American Scandal,"* CBS Television Miniseries, 2000.

Thomas Jefferson's portrait at the age of 61 (January, 1805) by the American painter Rembrandt Peale. At this time, Jefferson was in Washington, DC about to begin his second term as President, and the Lewis and Clark Expedition was well underway. Although the portrait was painted indoors, Jefferson is heavily bundled up to ward off the chill. He suffered greatly from cold weather most of his life, remarking in 1801, "Yet when I recollect on one hand all the sufferings I have had from cold, and on the other all my other pains, the former preponderate greatly." Back at Monticello, Madison Hemings, the son of Sally Hemings who claimed to be the son of Thomas Jefferson, is being born in this month.

The Jefferson-Hemings DNA Study

Herbert Barger, Jefferson Family Historian

I would like to address the issue of the Thomas Jefferson DNA Study and give my firsthand account regarding the misleading headline in the science journal *Nature,* dated November 5, 1998. That headline has had a very negative impact on the legacy of Thomas Jefferson and has raised many concerns regarding the rights of some Hemings descendants who claim Jefferson as an ancestor.

Before I discuss the current events surrounding the DNA study, I would like to provide a little historical background that might be useful in understanding this study.

Thomas Jefferson was born April 13, 1743, and lived on a plantation in Virginia known as Monticello. His wife, Martha Wayles Jefferson, died in 1782. Jefferson served as Ambassador to France from 1784 until 1789, when he returned home. While in France, he sent for his daughter, Polly, to be accompanied by Isabell, an older woman. That slave was unable to accompany Polly and, unbeknownst to Jefferson, Sally Hemings, who was around 14 years of age, was sent instead. Her brother James had been taken to France earlier with Jefferson to learn French cooking. Sally and her brother also returned to the United States with Jefferson and according to her son, Madison Hemings, she was pregnant when she returned and gave birth to a son in early 1790. According to another version of the story, this son's name was Tom, and he later took the name Tom Woodson. Sally had more children, Harriet born 1795 (died 1797), Beverly born 1798, perhaps a daughter born in 1799 (died in 1800), Harriet II born in 1801, Madison born in 1805, and Eston born in 1808 when Sally was 35 and Thomas Jefferson was 65.

James Callender was a reporter for a Richmond newspaper, *The Recorder,* and became a bitter enemy of Thomas Jefferson after Jefferson refused to appoint him as Postmaster in Richmond. In retaliation, Callender attacked President Jefferson in 1802 with the accusation that he had had a child, Tom, by one of his slaves, Sally Hemings. This accusation has been the source of controversy ever since. Callender has been described by some historians as one of the worst scandalmongers and character assassins in American history. Despite the accusations, Jefferson was reelected to a second term as President of the United States.

In 1997, an idea was conceived that might help shed some light on this long running rumor. This idea did not originate with the man that most people are led by the media to believe originated it. Dr. Eugene Foster, a retired pathologist, did help locate donors, did draw blood samples, and did personally deliver the samples to England; but the idea began with Mrs. Winifred Bennett, a friend of Dr. Foster's. She was convinced that by using the DNA Y chromosome, one could prove or disprove the rumors and accusations that Thomas Jefferson fathered the children of Sally Hemings. It was later realized that the study would be able to *disprove* the accusations but would *not* be able to *prove* the accusations.

The study results, together with additional research findings, were intended to be used for a book that Mrs. Bennett was in the process of writing. She asked Dr. Foster, a good friend, to help her perform the study. She would later come to realize that his actions and desire for fame would end both their relationship and the book project she was working on.

The plan was to compare the DNA of descendants of Thomas Jefferson, of Eston Hemings, of Thomas Woodson, and of the Carr brothers, Peter and Samuel, by using the Y chromosome found in DNA, which remains virtually unchanged from father to son. In order to perform this study, they needed to find descendants who came only from the male line, and therefore descendants of Thomas Jefferson's daughters would not be suitable. The theory was that if you could find a male line descendant of Thomas Jefferson whose Y chromosome matched the Y chromosome of a male line descendant of Eston Hemings and Thomas Woodson, then that would indicate that Thomas Jefferson's Y chromosome had been passed down through a relationship with Sally Hemings. However, this theory was imperfect because a match would not specify which Jefferson was the father—only some male member of the Jefferson family.

Thomas Jefferson had no male children by his wife that survived into adulthood and therefore no male line descendants. However, Dr. Foster and Mrs. Bennett were able to continue with the study by finding descendants of Thomas Jefferson's uncle, Field Jefferson, who would carry the same Y chromosome as Thomas Jefferson's father and grandfather. So the Y chromosome found in male line descendants of Field Jefferson would be the same as that found in male line descendants of Thomas, if he had any.

The reason for locating a descendant of the Carr brothers was because many people, including acknowledged Jefferson descendants, believed that one or both of the brothers was the father of one or more of Sally Hemings' children. However, there is no indication as to which of Sally's children they were supposed to have fathered. For this purpose, Dr. Foster and Mrs. Bennett were able to find descendants of the paternal grandfather of Peter and Samuel Carr.

As mentioned earlier, the theory that Mrs. Bennett and Dr. Foster were working to prove or disprove was not entirely valid. Thomas Jefferson had a brother named Randolph who lived nearby and had five sons. Thomas also had a cousin named George who carried the same Y chromosome. In the event that a match between a Hemings descendant and a Jefferson were found, there is absolutely no way to tell from which Jefferson it came, since it could have come from any one of the eight Jeffersons living near Monticello. Some people might argue that Jefferson DNA combined with historical information (rumors and oral history) point to Thomas; however, there are also good arguments to counter this theory.

Mrs. Bennett and Dr. Foster contacted the Thomas Jefferson Memorial Foundation (TJMF) to ask for help in locating descendants of Thomas Jefferson and the Carr brothers. The TJMF referred them to me since I had been studying Jefferson family history for more than 25 years. Much of my genealogical research has been donated to various libraries and also to The Monticello Association as well as to the TJMF.

I had become interested in family genealogy shortly after I retired from 27 years of military service. After my mother-in-law told me that she was somehow related to Thomas Jefferson, and after much research, I discovered that my wife, Evelyn, is a first cousin, six generations removed, of Thomas Jefferson. She descends from the line of Field Jefferson, Thomas' uncle, whose descendants donated blood to be used in the study.

I agreed to assist Dr. Foster after he contacted me, and I provided him with the names of several people who descended from Field Jefferson. I was also able to provide the name of someone who could give information on Sally Hemings' descendants, and I continued to provide additional research material throughout the course of the study.

Mrs. Bennett spent a lot of time searching through many old books and newspapers to locate the Woodson descendants and searched obituaries to locate some of the Carrs. When Dr. Foster made initial contact with the donors, they were not too eager to participate. I then made several calls to some of them to encourage their participation in this very important study.

With donors now consenting to give blood samples, the two were off visiting descendants, Dr. Foster drawing the samples and Mrs. Bennett interviewing the descendants for her book. There were nineteen subjects, which included five descendants of two sons of Field Jefferson, three descendants of three sons of the Carr brothers' grandfather, five descendants of two sons of Thomas Woodson, the alleged first son of Sally, one descendant of Eston Hemings, Sally's last child, and five control subjects. The blood samples were then hand-carried to England in December 1997 by Dr. Foster, to a laboratory for testing and comparison.

Later on, Mrs. Bennett and Dr. Foster discussed how and when to report their findings. Mrs. Bennett didn't want anything announced until after her book was published. She already had an agent who was enthusiastic about her book, but Dr. Foster was extremely eager to publish the results as soon as they were known. On several occasions he tried to convince her that publishing the results in a scientific journal would not hurt her book at all, "since nobody reads those journals anyway." In November 1998, much to her surprise, Mrs. Bennett read in the newspaper that he had published the results in *Nature*. He gave her little credit for her contribution to the study. She questioned why he would do such a thing by saying "Gene, what is it that you want? Do you want money?" He said "No, I want fame." A very hurt Mrs. Bennett said to me, "Well, he was just willing to sacrifice me for his fame." Needless to say, a friendship was ended.

While waiting for the results from the laboratory, I continued sending Dr. Foster historical information. Some of this information related to Thomas' brother Randolph, who lived about twenty miles away, Randolph's five sons, and other male Jeffersons who lived at or near Thomas Jefferson's home, Monticello. One of Randolph's sons, Isham, was "reared" by Thomas Jefferson according to the *History of Todd Co., Kentucky*. Dr. Foster responded by saying, "Thanks very much for the information about Isham and Randolph Jefferson. This is exactly the kind of information that will have to be considered if it turns out that the Jefferson Y chromosome is in the Hemings descendants. The DNA evidence in itself can't be conclusive for a variety of reasons. I look forward to the details you are sending." Dr. Foster indicated both interest and appreciation for this information and acknowledged its importance to the study. We both agreed that this information would have to be considered along with the laboratory results on the DNA. I also suggested to him that we should meet, along with other historians, and discuss the DNA findings and related historical information to determine how the results should be presented to the public.

I didn't want the public to come to the conclusion that Thomas Jefferson was the father without them knowing that other facts about the issue existed. I was worried that most people were unaware of Thomas' brother Randolph, his five sons, and other Jefferson male relatives who would have the same DNA as Thomas. Dr. Foster agreed that a meeting to discuss the presentation of the results would be a good idea. He received the results of the laboratory test in June 1998.

In late October 1998, however, Dr. Foster informed me that the results of the DNA test would be published in the next few days in the journal *Nature*, a science magazine published in England. There hadn't been any meeting between Dr. Foster, myself, or others (at least, not to my knowledge) to discuss the presentation of the results. The next week, *Nature* published an article written by Dr. Foster with the title "Jefferson Fathered Slave's Last Child." The article contained the following findings:

(1) There was no match between the DNA of descendants of Jefferson and Woodson. This finding was extremely important. It meant that Thomas Jefferson (or any other Jefferson) did not father Thomas Woodson as stated in Callender's 1802 article.

(2) There was no match between the DNA of Woodson, Hemings, and Carr descendants. This meant that neither of the Carr brothers fathered Thomas Woodson or Eston Hemings. However, it is still conceivable that they could have fathered one or more of Sally's other children.

(3) A match was found between the DNA of descendants of Field Jefferson and the descendant of Eston Hemings. This only means that any one of the Jefferson men previously mentioned could have fathered Eston Hemings, but it doesn't indicate which Jefferson.

In the article, Dr. Foster says that the purpose of the study was to prove or disprove whether the Carr brothers were the father. Since the Carr brothers were eliminated, the simplest explanation was that Thomas Jefferson fathered Eston Hemings. This may have been the simplest explanation, but to offer it as "the" explanation without explaining the rest of the story leads to a grossly incomplete and inaccurate conclusion. Dr. Foster's only caveat was that the DNA study was not conclusive. However, without explaining why the study was not conclusive and that there were other Jeffersons with access to Sally, the reader is left only with "the simplest explanation"—that it was Thomas Jefferson who was the father of Eston Hemings.

Needless to say I was extremely upset with the article and its misleading title. It implied that Thomas Jefferson was proven to be the father of Eston. I had given Dr. Foster significant amounts of historical information that should have been considered before any conclusion was reached. I could not believe that Dr. Foster would have allowed this article to be published with this title.

I later discovered that Dr. Foster and *Nature* had negotiated the headline for the simple DNA findings. Dr. Foster knew the title for the article would be "Jefferson Fathered Slave's Last Child." These are mighty powerful words to place on the name of President Thomas Jefferson and especially with no conclusive proof to back them up. Dr. Foster had previously informed me that, "Since I (Dr. Foster) am not a professional historian I don't have the training and skills needed to evaluate one item of historical evidence in the context of other evidence. So, I will continue to leave that to the historian and will read their opinions and conclusions with interest." Why, then, did he allow the conclusion, based on the DNA analysis, that Thomas Jefferson was the biological father of Eston Hemings? He knew for a fact that the DNA analysis alone could not conclusively prove that it was Thomas, and he knew of the existence of a number of other male Jeffersons that should have been considered.

None of the additional information I had provided him had been included in the article, which would have made it clear that Thomas was only one of eight or more Jeffersons who may have fathered Eston Hemings. I had believed, based on my many years of research, that it was possibly Randolph or one of his sons, Isham, who fathered Eston. Additional research leaves me even more convinced that it was Randolph. My concern was that the public would see the headline "Jefferson Fathered Slave's Last Child" and believe it to be historically and scientifically correct. I asked Dr. Foster why he allowed the article to run as it had, and why no meetings had been held. He said that *Nature* had put a rush on it, that they had placed limitations on how long the article would be, and that they were the ones who made up the title. *Nature,* however, stated that Dr. Foster knew very well what the title of the article was going to be.

To make matters worse, Drs. Joseph Ellis and Eric Lander wrote an accompanying article accepting the premise that Thomas Jefferson did indeed have an affair with Sally Hemings. I couldn't understand why *Nature,* a scientific journal, would be interested in publishing an article of an historical nature, particularly when they were placing limitations on how long a scientific article would be. Drs. Ellis and Lander state "Now, DNA analysis confirms that Jefferson was indeed the father of at least one of Hemings' children." How about the choice of such strong words as "confirms" and "indeed"? The public can easily be confused with this new DNA science and will actually believe the scientists and an award-winning historian, who had previously believed Thomas innocent of these charges. Professor Ellis has taken a 180-degree turn from his former beliefs on this issue. He previously stated, "In my judgment, the prospect of the relationship being true is remote." He is also quoted as saying, "Not because they say he was a gentleman and gentlemen do not do that sort of thing… But based on six years studying Jefferson, I believe his deepest sensual urges were directed at buildings rather than women."

Remember, there was *no* Jefferson/Woodson (alleged first child) match, thus, no long running "love affair." Even Professor Ellis, writing in *The New Republic,* December 31, 1998, had said there was no evidence what-soever that the Jefferson/Hemings liaison was a romance. He further made reference to an article written by Professor Sean Wilentz (who had recruited Professor Ellis to sign the full page article of historians in the *New York Times* of October 30, 1998), saying, "Professor Wilentz's 'Jefferson-Hemings romance' strikes me as fairy-tale stuff of the sappiest sort" and further, "Spinning the story that way plays to the popular crav-ing for a miniseries version of history…"

It should be noted that Professor Ellis didn't mention Randolph and sons in his Jefferson book and told me by phone on November 14, 1998, after the article had been published, that he knew nothing of Thomas' brother and nephews. Annette Gordon-Reed, author of *Thomas Jefferson and Sally Hemings: An American Controversy,* didn't mention Randolph and sons in her book either. Fawn Brodie, author of *Thomas Jefferson: An Intimate History,* mentioned Randolph as a ten year old and once as an adult. She did say Randolph was "less than mediocre in talent and native intelligence." I have to wonder whether these historians really knew of Randolph and his sons or not. It has been asserted that no one offered Randolph and his sons as an alternative to Thomas until after the DNA study results were published, and that they are now being offered in a desperate attempt to defend Thomas. I did in fact provide this information well in advance of the published results to Dr. Foster. It was the very information that Dr. Foster had said would be important if there were a Jefferson/Hemings match.

Randolph seemed to have been a private, non-political, fun-loving farmer who must have been well known by Jefferson's slave, Isaac, because years later he recalled that "Old Master's brother, Mass Randall was a mighty simple man: used to come out among black people, play the fiddle and dance half the night; hadn't much more sense than Isaac" (*Jefferson at Monticello*, by James A. Bear, Jr., University Press of Va. 1967, p. 22). It was probably Randolph that taught the Hemings men to play the fiddle, because Thomas was occupied in too many other pursuits for his country and at his two homes. He sometimes complained that he couldn't get to sleep because of the fiddle playing and noise in the slave quarters.

I have provided this information on Randolph and also have additional information on Thomas's first cousin, once removed, George Jefferson, Jr., educated by Thomas, and his agent and manager in Richmond, who must have come to Monticello to discuss business when Thomas came home. I don't suppose there would be any reason for Randolph to visit Monticello except when Thomas would come home. Could this possibly explain why Sally became pregnant only when Thomas was at Monticello? Yet, some refuse to acknowledge the importance of all the above information. I'll admit it does "muddy the water" a bit to know of seven other Jeffersons, any one of whom could have fathered Eston Hemings. But I feel this information is as plausible as any other oral or documented evidence presented.

I am just asking that it be written in history books for our future generations to learn, that "some" Jefferson fathered Eston Hemings. It cannot be *proven conclusively* that Thomas was the father. With all the "circumstantial evidence" that supports numerous other possibilities of who fathered Sally's children, I do not know how anyone can feel so adamant that Thomas had to be the father.

The American scientific journal, *Science,* came forward January 8, 1999, in an excellent article stating, "But now the authors of the report say the evidence for that [i.e., Thomas Jefferson fathered Eston] is less than conclusive." They make it abundantly clear that Dr. Foster now admits that the data establishes only that Thomas Jefferson was one of several candidates for the paternity of Eston Hemings. *Science* said that the Jefferson data has taken on a political spin and that Mr. Reed Irvine of Accuracy in Media (AIM) claims that the news media purposefully distorted the results of Dr. Foster's study. Also, in Annette Gordon-Reed's new updated version of her book *Thomas Jefferson and Sally Hemings: An American Controversy*, which includes an Author's Note on the DNA evidence, she states on page x, "The DNA test does not prove that the descendant of Eston Hemings was a direct descendant of Thomas Jefferson."

My study indicates to me that Thomas Jefferson was *not* the father of Eston or any other Hemings child. The DNA study, along with historical information, indicates possibly Randolph is the father of Eston and maybe the others. We do not know. Randolph was a widower and between wives when shortly after his wife's death, Sally became pregnant with her first child, Harriet I. It had been almost six years since she arrived at Monticello from Paris, thus, we can see that there was no "long term love affair" between Thomas and Sally. She continued having children until 1808 when Eston was born. Randolph Jefferson married his second wife the next year, 1809, and had a child, John, born about 1810. Three of Sally Hemings' children, Harriet, Beverly, and Eston (the latter two not common names), were given names of the family of Randolph Jefferson's mother, the Randolphs, after whom he was named.

Randolph was invited by Thomas to come to Monticello to visit him and Randolph's twin sister, who had arrived one day earlier. This was in August 1807, exactly nine months prior to Eston's birth. Randolph was also present at Monticello on May 27, 1808, exactly six days after Eston's birth on May 21. Thomas drafted Randolph's will on that date, and Randolph may also have come to see his son, Eston.

I encourage the media to come forward and gather the facts and present them to a most deserving public. I will be happy to provide more information if desired. Our children's history books must not be tarnished with inaccurate, misleading, and incomplete information, especially when other information is available but is being distorted to fit today's agendas. Thomas Jefferson must not be branded a hypocrite, a child rapist, a deadbeat dad, and other derogatory names just because all the information available was not considered in a scientific study.

After the articles appeared in the *Nature,* November 5, 1998, issue, the media went into a frenzy. Many newspapers and television news programs reported it had been conclusively proven that Thomas Jefferson had fathered a child by his slave. Within weeks, most of the world believed this to be fact, based on that headline in *Nature.* Dr. Foster wrote a follow-up article that appeared in the January 7, 1999, issue of *Nature* in which he explained that the DNA tests were not conclusive. This article received very little attention in the mainstream press however.

I believe that if the results of the DNA study had been properly presented, this issue would not be nearly as controversial as it is today. There is a great deal of historical evidence to consider before making a decision one way or the other, and even then, we cannot know with complete certainty. The TJMF issued a report in January 2000 concluding that Thomas Jefferson probably fathered one if not all of Sally Hemings' children. The truth is, they don't know. I informed Dr. Daniel P. Jordan, President of the TJMF, in October 1999, three months prior to the release of the TJMF Research Committee Report, that I had located a possible new source for DNA testing—the gravesite of a son of Madison Hemings. But Dr. Jordan did not take steps to obtain that very important piece of scientific data to match with the historical data, and he *did not* include this possibility in his report. The descendants of Madison's son, after first giving oral permission to obtain the DNA, later changed their minds, refused permission, and now state that they are happy with having only the oral history. Are you the reader happy about this cavalier attitude toward one of our Founding Fathers by the Monticello study group and the Madison descendants?

It is because of this inaccurate and misleading headline in the *Nature* article, the subjective conclusions reached by the TJMF, and the denial of valuable information to the public that a Scholars Commission was established by The Thomas Jefferson Heritage Society. This commission, composed of at least fourteen prominent professors and numerous specialists in various fields, has begun an exhaustive study of all information surrounding this issue. The public is entitled to a full and detailed report of their findings, and this could be issued as early as April 2001.

The gravesite marker of William Hemings, son of Madison Hemings and grandson of Sally Hemings, found by researcher Herbert Barger at Leavenworth National Cemetery, Kansas. William Hemings died in 1910, and it is believed his remains may contain usable DNA for Y-chromosomal testing. To date, the present-day Madison Hemings descendants have refused permission to disinter and test the remains.

Anatomy of a Media Run-Away
David Murray, Ph.D.
Director, Statistical Assessment Service

What do we know, for certain, regarding the relationship between Thomas Jefferson and his slave, Sally Hemings? For most Americans, following a barrage of media coverage, the following appears indubitable: Thomas Jefferson not only had a long-term sexual relationship with the young slave girl, he fathered at least one and most likely six children with her. All denials notwithstanding, Jefferson is not only inculpated but so are generations of American historians, who have steadfastly refused to grant credibility to the long-standing evidence found in the oral history of former slaves which attested to these facts.

And how do we now know these facts with certainty? It is because science has now demonstrated the truth of the circumstance, validating the oral claims with hard biological and statistical evidence. A clear-cut DNA finding buttressed with arcane probability calculations have together proven irrefutable. (Of course, since few of us actually read the evidence directly in the pertinent academic journals—*Nature* and *William and Mary Quarterly*, respectively—we actually know the facts only in their mediated form; that is, the news media so told us).

Not only is the science compelling, clear, and definitive, the academic community, we now read, has reached consensus on the issue—Jefferson did it. Are there still skeptics and resisters? Indeed, but they are not only inconsequential, they are suspect as to motive. Since the effect of the findings is a moral vindication for slave narratives (moreover, they affirm the sexual oppression of women), and hence, by extension, for the role of the entire African American community in American life, those who today resist the facts (or even express uncertainty) should be seen as not only benighted, but indeed, must be suspected of low motives.

The fact that researchers had found a genetic match between Thomas Jefferson's family line and the descendant of the last-born son of Sally Hemings (disclosed in the Nov. 5, 1998 issue of *Nature*) was, without doubt, the most heavily covered science story of 1998, with a second round of coverage extending into the year 2000. How did the press perform? Accounts contained strong assertions that paternity had been "proven," "conclusively demonstrated," or "resolved." Examples include:

- "DNA Link; Paternity Proved," the *Norfolk Virginian-Pilot*.
- "Adulterer on Mt. Rushmore," claimed the *Des Moines Register*, which included the charge of "statutory rape."
- "A boost for President Clinton in fighting impeachment... evidence proves Jefferson fathered at least one child by his slave," *CNN*.

National Public Radio's November 1 account was typical. Correspondent Daniel Zwerdling announced, "The proof is finally in. The president not only did have an illicit sexual affair, he fathered at least one child with his lover... DNA testing has ended (that) debate." *U.S. News & World Report* even ran a genealogical chart that showed a direct line between Jefferson and the modern descendant of Eston Hemings. Subsequent news reports after the initial episode continued with the firm sense of certainty, this time attached to a report issued by The Thomas Jefferson Memorial Foundation, notwithstanding objections and *caveats* expressed about the original DNA claim:

- "Jefferson Fathered Slave's Children, Foundation Says" *Chicago Tribune*
- "Jefferson's Secret Family: Foundation Backs Slave Ties" *Boston Globe*
- "Thomas Jefferson fathered one, if not all six, of slave Sally Hemings's children, the foundation that owns Monticello conceded." *Wall Street Journal*
- "Thomas Jefferson Was Father of Slave's Children" *Reuters*
- "After so many assertions, so many denials, so many years, it is now DNA-supported: Jefferson fathered at least one of Sally Heming's six children." *Washington Post*
- "There is no question something happened between Thomas Jefferson and his slave, Sally Hemings. Two years ago, a DNA study concluded that Jefferson was definitely the father of one and very likely all six of Hemings' children." *The New York Times*

This account in the *Times* was of particular interest, since they had previously published a letter (Nov. 9, 1998) from the actual author of the DNA study that specifically refuted this interpretation of his work. In the reporters' defense, it must be granted that "experts" were more than willing to egg them on to conviction. For instance,

- Mount Holyoke historian Joseph Ellis, appearing in Newsweek (Feb. 7, 1999): "For all intents and purposes, this ends the debate." Ellis also referred to Jefferson as a "white supremacist" in *The New Republic*.
- Archaeologist Fraser Neiman of The Thomas Jefferson Memorial Foundation in *USA Today* (Jan. 27, 1999): "The DNA evidence applies only to one child. This shows he, in all likelihood, fathered all six. Serious doubts about his paternity of all six children cannot reasonably be sustained."

Much of the coverage demonstrated a remarkable flight from careful and skeptical reporting. All too often, the news stories, commentary, and analysis transformed an intriguing but admittedly indeterminate scientific finding into a dead certainty. Several journalists went on to turn the DNA results into some sort of referendum on the current state of race relations and presidential politics. But what actually had been demonstrated? What the *Nature* article did by reporting a link between the Jefferson family and kin of Eston Hemings was to add enticing new evidence to a long-running historical debate. Before those findings, historians could only point to circumstantial evidence implicating Thomas Jefferson rather than one of his male-line relatives. The new DNA match with one descendant strengthens that circumstantial evidence. With these findings the balance shifts, suspicions become probabilities.

But certainty still eludes us. The best characterization of what has—and has not—been "proven" by the combination of circumstantial historical evidence and the DNA findings is found in the original *Nature* report, co-authored by retired pathologist Eugene Foster: "The simplest and most probable explanation for our molecular findings are that Thomas Jefferson, rather than one of the Carr brothers [sons of Jefferson's sister, not paternal-line carriers], was the father of Eston Hemings... We cannot completely rule out other explanations of our findings based on illegitimacy in various lines of descent." After the hyperbolic coverage began flourishing, Foster wrote his letter to the *New York Times* calling it "regrettable that [our] statement has been transmuted into assertions that all doubt had been removed." The letter also said, "The genetic findings my collaborators and I reported... do no prove that Thomas Jefferson was the father of one of Sally Heming's children. We never made that claim. Nor do we believe that the Y-chromosome type we found in Hemings's descendant occurs only in members of the Jefferson family... this study could not prove anything conclusively..."

The original *Nature* article contained ample warning signs that the certainty expressed by media may in fact be elusive. The Jefferson case, *Nature* pointed out, has always depended on the oral history of putative descendants and charges first lodged by political opponents in 1802 that Jefferson fathered the first-born son of Hemings, Thomas Woodson.

Descendants of Woodson were shown in *Nature* research to have no DNA match with Jefferson. Undaunted, *U.S. News* suggested that Jefferson might indeed be the father of Woodson, the DNA evidence having been lost through subsequent illegitimacy in the Woodson line. Jefferson defenders have used that same line of reasoning to explain away the presence of a Thomas Jefferson DNA match in the case of Eston Hemings. An additional qualifier is that Thomas Jefferson was 65 years old and Sally Hemings 37, rather than the 14-year-old ingénue of folklore, in the year that Eston was born. Thomas Jefferson himself was not tested, only descendants of his paternal uncle, Field Jefferson. This fact troubles forensic geneticists working professionally in DNA paternity cases with whom I consulted.

What did the DNA match positively establish? The findings show a probability that the DNA of Eston shows a descent from some male in the Jefferson paternal line, rather than being a randomly occurring match from someone in the general population, which is put at a 100-to-1 chance. A simple analogy would be recovering from a victim a bullet that has distinctive rifle-barrel markings enabling it to be traced. The research has shown that said rifle was owned by males of the Jefferson family. But who pulled the trigger? According to many forensic geneticists, to argue convincingly a paternity link in a modern court of law would require much higher odds against chance than 100-to-1.

The story broke the weekend before Election Day, and political as well as competitive forces appeared to drive the timing. *Nature* editors typically give reporters a few days' advance notice on research reports that appear in the magazine, though stories about those reports are normally embargoed until the date of the magazine's publication—in this instance, Thursday, Nov. 5, 1998. But, under pressure from news outlets that heard rumors of the findings and feared getting scooped, *Nature* agreed to the early release date of Friday, Oct. 30. That allowed the weekend papers and Monday editions of the newsweeklies to cover the controversy.

Accompanying the findings in *Nature* was a commentary by Joseph Ellis of Mount Holyoke College in Massachusetts, explicitly comparing the alleged actions of Jefferson to those of the current president. Some critics questioned the timing of the *Nature* publication. "Just two days before the election, the (DNA) story gave the everybody-does-it line both pedigree and prestige," wrote conservative columnist Charles Krauthammer. "Accident? Two days before that, a full-page ad appeared in the *New York Times* opposing Clinton's impeachment. Among the signers: the co-author of the article [Ellis] in *Nature* pronouncing the DNA data definitive, in which he noted wryly the Hemings report's 'impeccable timing.'" Foster, too, was troubled by the *Nature* commentary. He told the *Washington Times* on Nov. 10, "They unnecessarily politicized something that was intended to be a piece of scientific work."

The Memorial Foundation Report

The second round of news accounts of the affair was launched just days before the roll out of a lurid *CBS* sweeps-week miniseries. So what besides the dubious imperative of ratings drove the news in January 2000, including a front-page, above the fold, full color portrait story in ·*USA Today* (Jan. 27)? Was there new science? No; the same indeterminate DNA study remained just as inconclusive as before. Was there additional evidence? Not really; archeologist Neiman had put statistical form to a thesis already well established since 1968, that Thomas Jefferson had been at Monticello during plausible times that Sally conceived. Was there new documentation or testimony? None. Since the evidentiary landscape hadn't changed since 1998, why the dramatic coverage? The immediate rationale was that the Foundation that owns Monticello had assembled scholarly parties who conceded that Thomas Jefferson likely had fathered not one, not two, but all six of Sally's children. It became apparent to anyone following the actual evidentiary trail that more was going on here than strict science; in some measure, Thomas Jefferson had become a contested national symbol on a battlefield of the current culture war, his behavior being treated by media and by many scholars as an implicit referendum on race, gender, and Clintonian politics. Some news accounts made this moral narrative quite explicit:

- From *Newsweek:* "(Hemings' descendants were) proud to claim a slave as an ancestor, along with a president. In that sense, at least, the country has made some progress toward the ideal of equality that Jefferson embraced in his philosophy, even as he failed to embody it in his life."

- Family member Lucian Truscott IV was quoted in several stories as saying, "This is like the Civil Rights Act for the Hemings family…this report is the emancipation of the Hemings."

- *Reuters* declared, "The confirmation of a direct link between one of the country's founding fathers and generations of black claimants to his name symbolically affirms the central role of African-Americans in the making of the modern nation."

- *Washington Post* letter, Feb. 3; by Trena Woodson: "Monticello now supports the history my family has maintained despite historians and white America trying to deny the relationship to protect Jefferson… Maybe now African Americans will gain the respect that African American history is strong and truthful and that we played an important role in building this country."

While it must be a disappointment to the author of this letter, who wrote in defense of her ancestor, Thomas Woodson, it must be remembered that the only clear conclusion that the DNA evidence did reach was that Thomas Woodson could *not* be Thomas Jefferson's offspring, nor indeed that of *any* Jefferson male. That is, those who denied the relationship of Woodson to Thomas Jefferson were correct, and the oral history of the Woodson family, which included the claim that Woodson bore a striking physical resemblance to the president, was erroneous on all counts.

Moreover, the scenario of Thomas Jefferson and the 14-year-old Sally Hemings having sex in Paris was conjectured largely on the basis of the Woodson claim, which has now been shown to be in error. Surely we learn from this episode the danger in having the true and important role of African Americans in "building this country" hinge on a contingent scientific result and dubious oral history. As for those who had the bad form to remain skeptical, their failing was soon characterized as more than cognitive—it was morally obtuse. For example, E. M. Halliday, former editor in chief of *American Heritage* magazine (editorial, *New York Times* Jan. 8, 1999) was particularly dismissive of those who do not find the argument convincing, ridiculing "the extremes to which the true disbelievers are driven in their fervor to exonerate our third president from charges of miscegenation… Well, there's always the Man in the Moon, who if you're given to far-out fantasy might imaginably be a Jefferson. But it doesn't seem too probable."

As the *New York Times* characterized those who found the argument weak (in the headline of the Halliday piece), they are "Hemings-Jefferson Deniers, Desperate." Suspicion that "deniers" was a deliberately loaded term has been strengthened by commentators such as Chris Myers, whose letter to the *Washington Post* (May 13, 2000) stated, "Like the Holocaust deniers and others… Jefferson's purported defenders have a problem with the truth." Yet it would appear, based on evidence and arguments supported in this volume, that a straightforward concern for accurate history may be a sufficient foundation for questioning the received media opinion.

In a manner that has by now become typical, the actual Report from Monticello for reporters who read through it, was more qualified and less certain than news accounts purporting to discuss it. Interestingly, the Monticello Report offered comments from distinguished outside scientists about the DNA evidence. But a glance at their actual testimony reveals a fair amount of caution and hedging. After all, Thomas Jefferson was never tested, a fact reporters almost universally ignore. Rather, the analysis was of Sally's great great grandson, John Jefferson, 53, who was matched with blood of contemporary descendants of Thomas Jefferson's paternal uncle, Field Jefferson with a probability of 1 in 100. As DNA author Foster put it in the *Washington Times* (Nov. 10, 1998), "The odds of this coming from someone *other than a Jefferson* (emphasis added) are no more than one in one hundred." That is, the odds show that one out of every 100 random tests of strangers in Virginia could be expected to produce a match. Showing that Thomas Jefferson was the source of the DNA is simply beyond the capacity of the study.

No wonder that the "corroborating" scientists in the Report were much more circumspect than the journalists. What did the scientists who submitted reports actually say? Dr. Kenneth Kidd, a professor of genetics at Yale observed, "I think Eric Lander and Joseph Ellis (authors of the *Nature* 1998 commentary) over-interpreted the results as proving that Jefferson was the father of Eston… The Y chromosome data do not prove that Thomas Jefferson himself was the ancestor of Eston, but that is certainly one of the likely specific scenarios within the "identical by descent" family of explanations…a male line relative quite remotely related to President Thomas Jefferson would likely have the same Y chromosome as Jefferson (for example, J41 and J49 are fifth cousins once removed and have the same Y chromosome). The data do prove that Thomas Woodson was *not* the son of Thomas Jefferson or any close male-line relative of Jefferson….As with modern day paternity testing, we can prove that a man is not/was not the father, but we cannot absolutely prove a man is/was the father…so the proof ultimately rests on demonstrating that Thomas Jefferson was present at the time Eston was conceived and that no other male relative with the same Y chromosome was hiding in the bushes…the authors are right when they say these results…are at least 100 times more likely if Thomas Jefferson is Eston's father than if someone unrelated to Thomas Jefferson was the father…it is also correct to say 'these results for Eston are at least 100 times more likely if Thomas Jefferson's cousin is Eston's father…'"

The consequences of the media rush to judgment are hardly benign. To enlist the facts of Jefferson as a sort of perverse character witness in the presidential scandal of 1998 is to subordinate the purposes of science to the dubious and shifting needs of politics. Just as troubling is the implication in some media reports that blacks in America should be somehow pinning their standing in America's destiny on the outcome of DNA tests. By making science submit to our desires to satisfy our political or racial hopes, we ultimately damage the capacity to understand ourselves.

But beyond harm done to science, it is demeaning to Jefferson and Hemings to make their role in our shared destiny a matter of genetic contingency. What if today's (or tomorrow's, for that matter) DNA facts had shown otherwise? Should African Americans be regarded as historically diminished? In fact, isn't our insistent preoccupation with the body, rather than concerns of the spirit and the character, precisely how we have impeded our racial understanding?

The contest over Thomas Jefferson's paternity will in all probability go on. But as the debate continues, we hope that blacks and whites, searching for our common American bond, continue to seek kinship in Jefferson's ideals as earnestly as it has been sought in our genetics.

A Primer on Jefferson DNA

John H. Works, Jr.

DNA

DNA is material within the cell that governs the inheritance of eye color, hair color, stature, bone density, and many other human and animal traits.

Persons Tested

Since Thomas Jefferson himself had no known male descendants (his wife Martha bore six children between 1772 and her death in 1782, but only two daughters lived to adulthood), a direct comparison between his and Sally Hemings' offspring could not be made. Dr. Eugene Foster, a retired University of Virginia pathologist, therefore analyzed DNA from other male members of the Jefferson clan and compared them with samples from Sally Hemings' male descendants to see if a Jefferson fathered them.

Dr. Foster conducted DNA tests on five male line descendants of two sons of Thomas Jefferson's paternal uncle, Field Jefferson, and five male line descendants of two sons of Thomas Woodson (1790–1879), Sally Hemings' supposed first child, one male line descendant of Eston

(1808–1852), Sally Hemings' last child, and three male line descendants of three sons of John Carr (grandfather of Samuel and Peter Carr, who were Jefferson's nephews), long thought by the acknowledged Thomas Jefferson descendants to have been responsible for fathering Sally Hemings' children. For good measure, a panel of white descendants of Monticello's neighbors were also tested in case their forefathers might have contributed to Sally Hemings' offspring.

Uncommon DNA Haplotype

According to Dr. Foster, the average frequency of microsatellite haplotypes in the general population is estimated to be about 1.5%, and the specific Jefferson family microsatellite haplotype has never been observed outside the Jefferson family. It was not found among a sample of 670 European men or more than 1,200 worldwide.

Nonspecific DNA Results Link "Some" Jefferson

Dr. Foster found that there was a match between the male descendants of Uncle Field Jefferson and those of Sally Hemings' youngest son, Eston Hemings. However there was no match between the male descendants of Tom Woodson, Sally Hemings' supposed first-born son, and any of the others tested. The Carr descendants also did not match any of the others, and neither did the neighbors' descendants. Dr. Foster concluded that "the simplest and most probable explanation for our molecular findings are that Thomas Jefferson, rather than one of the Carr brothers, was the father of Eston Hemings Jefferson, and that Thomas Woodson was not Thomas Jefferson's son."

Eight Jeffersons Could Have Been the Father of Eston

This DNA study testing the Y chromosome found that there was a link to "some" Jefferson, but not necessarily Thomas, having been the father of Eston, Sally Hemings' youngest son. These DNA tests, plus the historical data, indicate that any one of eight Jeffersons could have been the father of Eston and there was nothing in the scientific evidence alone to indicate it was Thomas rather than one of the others. The eight possibilities suggested by the DNA tests in conjunction with the historical data are

Thomas, Randolph (T. Jefferson's brother), Randolph's five sons, and a cousin George. Since no one has ever denied that it was likely that "some" Jefferson-related male fathered Sally Hemings' children, these recent DNA tests only provide more certainty to what we already knew or suspected. And since the only available DNA evidence comes from direct male line descendants of persons who have descended from a common male line with Thomas Jefferson (father, grandfather, etc.), the test is inherently nonspecific. The same Y chromosome existed in Mr. Jefferson's brother Randolph, who lived 20 miles from Monticello, and in five of Randolph's sons, who were in their teens or 20s when Sally Hemings was having children, as well as in one cousin who was known to have visited, and even in several other cousins who might have visited Monticello, but about whom no record of visitation is available.

Misleading Headline—"Jefferson Fathered Slave's Last Child"

On November 5, 1998, the journal *Nature* placed an inaccurate and misleading headline based on this study which read, "Jefferson Fathered Slave's Last Child." Most of the mass media assumed the headline to be correct. At the time, Daniel P. Jordan, Ph.D. and President of the Thomas Jefferson Memorial Foundation (TJMF), stated that "Dr. Foster's DNA evidence indicates a sexual relationship between Thomas Jefferson and Sally Hemings." Subsequently Mr. Jordan admitted that "after the initial rush to conclusions came another round of articles explaining that the study's results were less conclusive than had earlier been reported." Dr. Foster also later admitted that "it is true that men of Randolph Jefferson's family could have fathered Sally Hemings' later children. The title assigned to our study was misleading in that it represented only the simplest explanation of our molecular findings: namely, that Thomas Jefferson, rather than one of the Carr brothers, was likely to have been the father of Eston Hemings Jefferson. We know from the historical and the DNA data that Thomas Jefferson can neither be definitely excluded nor solely implicated in the paternity of illegitimate children with his slave Sally Hemings."

New Woodson DNA Tests

DNA tests performed on one Eston line came up positive, but tests performed originally on five Woodson lines in November 1998 came up negative, as did a DNA test on a sixth line performed in March 2000. These results should demonstrate beyond any reasonable doubt that Thomas Jefferson was not the father of Tom Woodson. The Woodson DNA tests are important because if Tom Woodson was Sally Hemings' Paris-conceived son and could be shown to have Jefferson DNA, it would then be almost certain that Thomas Jefferson was his father, since Thomas was the only Jefferson in Paris at the time who could have impregnated Sally. Although the Woodson family still claims descent from Thomas Jefferson, they seem to have lost interest in the Jefferson family cemetery. The Thomas C. Woodson Family Association declined to attend The Monticello Association's Annual Business Meeting held on Sunday, May 7, 2000. The Woodson Family Association's President, Robert Golden, stated that the care of the Jefferson family cemetery and possible burial there "is not of interest to the Woodson Family Association itself but might be of interest only to specific individuals within the Woodson family."

Grave of William Hemings Located

After an exhaustive 18-month search, Herbert Barger, Jefferson family historian and genealogist, located the grave of William Hemings, the son of Madison Hemings and the grandson of Sally Hemings, in the Leavenworth National Cemetery in Kansas. Nevertheless, the Madison Hemings branch of the family decided not to press forward with DNA testing.

This particular scientific inquiry on the Madison Hemings branch would be interesting because results from the DNA tests should confirm one of three things: (i) if there is no match then their claim that Madison is a descendant of Thomas Jefferson would be invalid (and this would fall into the same category as the Woodson oral history, for which DNA indicated there was no Jefferson/Woodson match), (ii) it could show a Carr/Madison descendant match, thus the claim would be valid that one of the Carr brothers is the father of Sally's children (at least for Madison), or (iii) as in the case of Madison's brother, Eston, who was found to have a match with "some" Jefferson descendant (not necessarily Thomas), this match could duplicate that finding. However, a match with "some" Jefferson would still not rise to the level of clear and convincing evidence that is required under current applicable paternity laws, since any one of eight Jeffersons could have been the father of Madison and there would be nothing to indicate it was Thomas. Such a study would, however, significantly advance scientific understanding of the Hemings paternity issues.

The William Hemings grave site has long been forgotten by other Hemings family members. At first the Hemings claimed not to know its location. Then the Hemings questioned whether this was really William's grave, until Mr. Barger provided irrefutable evidence. The question naturally arises, if the Hemings oral histories are so authoritative, why didn't they know where their ancestors were buried? One of the first, most basic things a family does is honor the burial place of their ancestors. That comes before any elaborate oral tradition. Native Americans have a very rich oral history culture. They know where their sacred grounds are and where their burial grounds are over several generations. It is sometimes risky to cross from one culture to another, but it seems safe to say that honoring family burial places is a near universal human trait. Some cultures, such as in India, cremate their dead and scatter the ashes, but it would be difficult to find a culture that buries their dead and then ignores the grave sites of their ancestors. This failure to retain as part of their oral tradition the burial site of a relative calls into question the strength and validity of the family oral history of the descendants of Madison Hemings.

DNA Testing of Acknowledged Descendants

The current members of The Monticello Association are all descendants of persons who were acknowledged by Thomas Jefferson as his offspring, and no acknowledged descendant of Thomas Jefferson need be tested for a DNA match under current paternity standards.

A human being's DNA exists as 23 pairs of chromosomes. In male descendants, all of those chromosome pairs change with every generation except the Y chromosome in the 23rd, because each generation represents the coming together of a male and a female, and that results in a new combination at each conception. When testing for paternity, there are therefore two different kinds of tests that can be run. A son's entire 23 pairs of chromosomes can be tested to determine whether the son is the product of his father. This test will be specific to the father, and any other male in his family (other than an identical twin) will not yield the same result. Father and grandson (or any other lineal descendant) will not produce the same result, because although the Y chromosome will be the same for all direct male-line descendants of the grandfather, all the other chromosomes will have changed, since in each instance the male descendant combines with a new mother and that produces new combinations. If the test is run on the Y chromosome component only, the result will reveal whether the male has the same Y chromosome as other direct male-line descendants, but that result will not indicate which male out of all the male-line descendants is the father. The result will only reveal that "some" male out of all those male-line descendants is the father.

The blood and DNA tests conducted in the Jefferson-Hemings controversy can only be carried out on samples of the male Y chromosome because it passes unchanged from father to son. Since Thomas Jefferson's son died in infancy and he only had daughters who lived to maturity, it is impossible to definitively link any descendant of Thomas Jefferson to Thomas Jefferson himself using DNA alone. (This would be true even if Thomas Jefferson did have male descendants. Such male descendants would only have the Jefferson Y chromosome, which does not establish a specific link to Thomas. The presumptive link, of course, would be very persuasive.) Recent researchers seeking to discover a match with the Hemings line could sample only direct male line descendants of persons who have descended from a common male line with Thomas Jefferson (i.e., his grandfather). If the acknowledged descendants of Thomas Jefferson submitted to DNA testing the test would be futile because the only genetic test that could be performed would be on the Y chromosome. The acknowledged descendants of Thomas Jefferson are all descended through Thomas Jefferson's daughter, not the male line. Thus they would have the Y chromosome from their male lines, which is not the same Y chromosome as any Jefferson. For example, a son of Martha would have the Randolph Y chromosome, and any direct male descendant would have that same Randolph Y chromosome. Therefore it is impossible that any descendant of Thomas Jefferson's daughters would have the Jefferson Y chromosome (unless some descendant along the line later married a male line descendant of Field Jefferson). Since all of the descendants of Thomas Jefferson's daughters had Y chromosomes from male lines other than the Jeffersons, nothing could be more futile than to test the acknowledged descendants of Thomas Jefferson.

Exhumation of Thomas Jefferson

If Thomas Jefferson were exhumed for Y chromosome DNA testing it would only confirm that he carried the same Y chromosome as the other seven Jeffersons in question. The only way this would not be true is if Thomas Jefferson were illegitimate. Besides being futile, it is very unlikely that there would be usable DNA that could be tested after so many years.

Illegitimacy

The genetic trail of any of the descendants tested could have been broken in subsequent generations if any of the mothers in the presumed chain had her son by a man outside the assumed male line. One of the lines of descendants from Tom Woodson actually demonstrated such a broken genetic trail, apparently due to an illegitimate union in a later generation. Some of the Hemings' lines cannot be tested, as there are no male line descendants.

DNA and Legal Requirements of Paternity

There is no reason to use DNA testing if the father acknowledges paternity.

In the absence of the father acknowledging paternity the law has determined that the most reliable way of determining paternity is blood and DNA testing, and there are clear rules one must follow to establish paternity. The responsibility for obtaining these rights and providing appropriate legal evidence belongs solely to the Hemings descendants and the burden of proof lies with them, not with The Monticello Association.

Since the law recognizes blood or DNA tests as the most reliable method in order to determine paternity in case of disputes, oral history plays no part and most other information is irrelevant as to whether someone is a lineal descendant for purposes of the right of burial in The Monticello Association graveyard. While interesting, the oral history promoted by the Hemingses plays absolutely no part when it comes to determining their rights as heirs of Thomas Jefferson. Family oral history may be useful in a scientific investigation as a pointer to suggest lines of inquiry, or to support other, more substantial evidence, but it cannot serve as the only means to establish paternity.

From a legal standpoint admissibility is the test which determines whether the evidence may be considered, e.g., it is information from a source which the law permits in a legal proceeding and is material and relevant to the issues presented, and depending on the nature of the evidence, it can be determined whether greater or lesser weight should be accorded to it. Hearsay is testimony offered by someone who does not have personal knowledge that the testimony is true. A witness cannot be cross-examined on hearsay because the witness only knows what he has been told. For that reason, hearsay is inadmissible unless it falls within certain limited exceptions. Oral history is inherently hearsay and therefore inadmissible. Hence, oral history cannot be used to establish paternity.

A Committee Insider's Viewpoint

White McKenzie Wallenborn, M.D.

In December 1998, Daniel Jordan, the president of the Thomas Jefferson Memorial Foundation (TJMF), appointed a nine person in-house committee to evaluate the DNA study that had just been reported by Dr. Eugene Foster in the journal *Nature*. Dr. Foster's article revealed that a descendant of Sally Hemings' fifth child, Eston, had a Y chromosome haplotype which was identical to the Y chromosome haplotype of five descendants of Field Jefferson, an uncle of Thomas Jefferson. The committee was asked to review all of the pertinent information related to the Jefferson-Hemings controversy and recommend how this new information should be incorporated into the historical interpretation at Monticello.

This commentary is the personal view of one of the committee members and is compiled from materials that were provided to all committee members and from my personal experiences.

The committee was chaired by Dianne Swann-Wright, who had been at Monticello since 1993 when she was hired to help with the "Getting Word" project. This was a program whose purpose was to try to interview and record the oral histories of the descendants of Monticello slaves. Dianne, an African-American, had recently received her Ph.D. in History from the University of Virginia. Lucia (Cinder) Stanton, Shannon Senior Research Historian, had an undergraduate degree from Radcliffe College. She had been employed at Monticello for over twenty years, had written many reports and booklets, including some on slavery at Monticello, and was very knowledgeable. She was most likely the principal author of the TJMF Research Committee's Final Report.

For about three years prior to the report, both Dianne and Cinder had expressed private opinions that Thomas Jefferson was the father of Sally Hemings' children. Camille Wells, who had recently been employed at Monticello to head the Research Department (and who later resigned from that position and is no longer at Monticello), was a member of the committee also. Fraser Neiman, director of the Archaeology Department at Monticello, who had been at Monticello for about four years, and who had been previously at Stratford, the Virginia birthplace of General Robert E. Lee, as archaeologist, was an appointed member. Whitney Espich, Communications Officer at Monticello (who also resigned from Monticello during the summer of 2000), was in charge of media evaluation for the committee. Elizabeth Dowling Taylor, former Head Guide at Monticello (who has since resigned from Monticello), was also on the committee. Elizabeth had a Ph.D. in Genetics from the University of Virginia but never worked in that field as far as I know. She was an extremely good Head Guide, demanded that accurate and verifiable information be provided by the guides, and arranged many excellent programs and conferences for Monticello. Nevertheless, she apparently told the last class of guides that she trained that they were to say that Thomas Jefferson was the father of Sally Hemings' children, and this was before the DNA Study Committee had finished its analysis and reached their conclusions. For the last two years of her tenure as Head Guide, she asked the guides to dramatically increase their tour presentation of slavery throughout the house. Anne Porter, an experienced educator, was an education guide for Monticello, handling mostly children's tours and programs for Monticello. Dave Ronka, also a well-trained educator and now on the faculty at Piedmont Community College, was and still is a house guide at Monticello. I, White McKenzie (Ken) Wallenborn, was trained by the United States Air Force as a statistician prior to my entering medical school at the University of Virginia. I was on the faculty of the University of Virginia School of Medicine for 33+ years, retiring as Clinical Professor. I did basic research at the University for nine years. In addition, I also had a private practice at the Martha Jefferson Hospital in Charlottesville, Virginia, for 33+ years. After retiring, I became a guide at Monticello for five years, resigning in March 2000. I had also been appointed to the committee.

Just as our committee was starting our deliberations, Dianne Swann-Wright asked me if I had read Annette Gordon-Reed's book, *Thomas Jefferson and Sally Hemings: An American Controversy*. I said that I had only read several chapters in the book and wasn't particularly impressed with it. She asked me to read the entire book which I did prior to the end of January 1999. I was not sure why she wanted me to read that book and why she did not ask me whether I had read other books, such as Dumas Malone's or Alf Mapp's or Merrill Peterson's. It did not take long to figure it out, however, as the committee's study outline seemed to be taken almost directly from Annette Gordon-Reed's book. And by the way, Dianne Swann-Wright, Cinder Stanton, and Annette Gordon-Reed have been the closest of friends, both before and since the DNA Study Committee Report was released.

After the committee was a little less than one third of the way through our deliberations, I went to see Dan Jordan, the President of the TJMF. The reason was that I had become very upset at what was happening in the committee. I informed him that there were not many friends of Thomas Jefferson on this committee, and that the committee had already reached their conclusions. Further, I told him that I sensed a strong power play aimed at the TJMF to force them to accept something that was politically correct and not historically accurate. Mr. Jordan said that he would make a note of this, but that I should stay on the committee, which I did.

As the committee began to throw out most of the evidence that would exonerate Mr. Jefferson, it became even more obvious that they were following Annette Gordon-Reed's lead, since this was the same tactic that she had used in her book. For example, in Thomas Jefferson's letter to Robert Smith in which he acknowledged the Walker affair but stated that this was the only one of "their allegations" founded in truth, the committee threw this out stating that the letter was ambiguous, as they did not know what the other allegations were. The majority of the committee then proceeded to dismiss the other eyewitness accounts because they were "problematic."

I agree that there is significant historical evidence that would show that Thomas Jefferson could have been the father of Eston Hemings, but I also feel strongly that there is significant historical evidence of equal stature that indicates that Thomas Jefferson was *not* the father of Eston (or any of Sally Hemings' children). These events happened more or less two hundred years ago, and only four or possibly five people (Thomas Jefferson, Sally Hemings, Randolph Jefferson, Peter Carr, and maybe Samuel Carr) would have known the truth about the paternity question. Only one of them has left us direct evidence in his own words and handwriting, and that was Thomas Jefferson himself. None of the others who would have had firsthand knowledge of the facts have put down statements in their own handwriting and their own words.

On July 1, 1805, Thomas Jefferson wrote a cover letter to Robert Smith, Secretary of the Navy, and enclosed a copy of a letter to Mr. Levi Lincoln, the Attorney General. In this cover letter, Mr. Jefferson pled guilty to one of the Federalist charges: that when young and single, he offered love to a handsome lady. He acknowledged the incorrectness of the act but said that it was the only one founded in truth among all their allegations against him. Jefferson's statement has got to be a very straightforward denial of all the Federalist charges, which included the report of a sexual liaison with Sally Hemings (i.e., that he had fathered Sally Hemings' children). Some feel that this statement is ambiguous, but how can it be? Mr. Jefferson and his cabinet members, Robert Smith and Levi Lincoln, certainly knew all of the Federalist charges against the President. Thomas Jefferson was not known to issue falsehoods to his intimate associates. I believe this statement by Thomas Jefferson is a significantly powerful denial. Ms. Stanton quotes Joanne Freeman as saying Mr. Jefferson had an elastic conception of the truth, when he believed the stakes for the nation were high. We are not talking about the stakes for the nation here, but the private communication between Thomas Jefferson and two of his close personal and political friends. There is no proof that I am aware of that would show that Mr. Jefferson told anything but the truth to any of his adult family, friends, or close political associates.

Ms. Stanton also states: "We know Jefferson's rationalizing talents and can imagine ways he could find a fairly comfortable place for this relationship in his view of himself." This statement belies all of Mr. Jefferson's professions of morality, his assertions that a slave master must not abuse those under his control, and especially his strong and well-known feelings about miscegenation. An even less scholarly comment was proposed by Ms. Stanton: that Jefferson might have considered a sexual liaison with a slave necessary for his health, as he had books on the subject of health and sexual activity. This is preposterous! In my library are books by Fawn Brodie and Annette Gordon-Reed, but by no means do I agree with them nor should anyone make a supposition that I do just because they are in my collection. Thomas Jefferson himself never wrote about or was quoted as saying anything that would give credence to these statements.

Edmund Bacon (born March 28, 1785, near Monticello) had the title of overseer at Monticello from September 29, 1806, until about October 15, 1822 (sixteen years). Edmund Bacon was interviewed at length (for several weeks) by the Rev. Hamilton Wilcox Pierson, president of Cumberland College, Princeton, Kentucky, around 1861 or 1862, at Mr. Bacon's home. Bacon also shed some light on the Sally Hemings controversy. He said that Thomas Jefferson was not the father of Sally's daughter (Harriet), because he saw someone other than Thomas Jefferson coming out of her mother's room. Mr. Bacon recalled that he went to live with Mr. Jefferson on Dec. 27, 1800, and was with him precisely twenty years. But Mr. Jefferson recorded his employment as overseer for sixteen years. Possibly Mr. Bacon had started working as early as age sixteen but was not hired as overseer until age twenty, and if so would have been working at Monticello when Harriet Hemings was conceived and born. If Bacon had actually come to live at Monticello at age sixteen, on December 27, 1800 (before Thomas Jefferson was inaugurated for his first term as president), he would have been working at Monticello during the time of conception and birth of Sally Hemings' last three children—Harriet, Madison, and Eston.

Bacon's observations are certainly valid information and strongly suggest that another male was having a sexual liaison with Sally Hemings. In Thomas Jefferson's Farm Book and Garden Book there are at least two references to Bacon having several jobs at Monticello before he became overseer in 1806. His father had apparently done some contract jobs for Mr. Jefferson, and so Edmund Bacon was known to Mr. Jefferson well before 1806. But whether or not he was at Monticello at Harriet's or Madison's conception is not nearly as important as his observation that Sally's male companion was *not* Thomas Jefferson. There are no secrets on a farm, and Monticello was no different, so Edmund Bacon would have been aware of who was having an affair with Sally Hemings, even if the affair had been going on before Bacon's arrival.

But Ms. Stanton says: "First we have to consider reasons Bacon might have had for absolving Jefferson of the Hemings connection (he was talking to a clergyman in 1860, when mores were decidedly different from those of 1800; he was deeply loyal to Jefferson and proud of his association with a great man, and so forth)." Of course the main reason Bacon had for absolving Mr. Jefferson was that he was telling the truth about the situation! As to the mores being different in 1860 from those of 1800, it is doubtful that telling a truism (or a falsehood) to a clergyman in 1860 would be different from telling one in 1800. And what would be wrong with being proud of your association with a great man as long as you are willing to tell the truth about him? There just is no good reason for Mr. Bacon to tell lies during his interview.

Thomas Jefferson Randolph emphatically denied that Mr. Jefferson had commerce with Sally or any other of his female slaves. He also told historian Henry S. Randall that Sally Hemings was the mistress of Peter, and that her sister Betsy (she was actually the daughter of Sally's half sister) was the mistress of Samuel Carr. Actually, the DNA evidence may have strengthened Thomas Jefferson Randolph's version of the events. The DNA applies only to Eston Hemings and not to Sally Hemings' other four children and in no way eliminates Peter or Samuel Carr from being the father of those four children.

Ms. Stanton made the statement that "we know, however, from the Memorandum Books and other sources that Jefferson was at Monticello at the right time to father all of Sally Hemings' children." But Sally Hemings' presence at Monticello is not accurately recorded and her presence or absence cannot be proven as also coinciding with Mr. Jefferson's presence. And because it is impossible to determine the timing of the presence or absence of other males with the Jefferson DNA haplotype at Monticello, we have no way to compare the probability of their being the father of Sally Hemings' children with the probability that Thomas Jefferson was the father. The evidence just is not there for vital comparison studies.

There are some striking coincidences which also add to the perplexity. For example, when Jefferson finally came home after his second term as President, for some reason Sally quit having children. Randolph Jefferson (TJ's brother and a possible father of Eston) was widowed, probably as early as 1796, but as soon as he remarried in late 1808 or early 1809, Sally had no more children. Thomas Jefferson, Jr. (Randolph's son and a possible father of Eston) married on Oct. 3, 1808, and after this date, Sally had no more children. Obstetrical calculations are notoriously fallible and, coupled with early or late deliveries being entirely possible, throw more doubt on statistical studies based on these factors. At any rate, Neiman's statistical study of Thomas Jefferson's presence cries out for valid comparative studies of the other Jefferson males who might have fathered Eston, and in the absence of these comparisons, the results are inconclusive. Because no accurate records were kept of these other Jefferson male visits to Monticello, no comparisons can be performed. And given the fact that there is no proof of Sally Hemings' presence at Monticello when Eston was conceived, the picture really becomes muddled.

Madison Hemings' recollections lack credibility because of the language used, and Wetmore's "Memoirs of Madison Hemings" might have harmed his case because of the use of journalistic license. Madison Hemings admittedly had no formal education, but in the memoirs, Wetmore has Madison using an amazing vocabulary and grammar, and having a remarkable knowledge of history. All of this was remembered some thirty-five or forty years after he was at Monticello. Wetmore's use of direct quotes instead of paraphrasing would have helped make the memoirs more believable. As far as I can tell, Wetmore's handwritten notes covering his interview have not been found, and as a result it is hard to tell when the words were Madison's or Wetmore's.

Wetmore's article about Madison Hemings cannot be called an "accurate reflection of Hemings' statements" as there are no direct statements of Madison Hemings before and/or subsequent to the publication that reaffirm Wetmore's opinions. To say his article is accurate without access to Wetmore's interview notes just is not acceptable. Madison Hemings did not sign the original document, or at least there is no record of a signature to affirm concurrence with Wetmore's version. There can be no doubt that the language is Wetmore's and whether or not he changed the content to fit his own strong political agenda is unknown, but becomes suspect. In other words, this document is very problematic and should not be considered as a primary source of evidence. Ms. Stanton comments that "the details of language and historical facts are irrelevant to the main issue: paternity." But the entire questionable composition of Wetmore's publication, coupled with the fact that Madison never acknowledged the source of his information as to who his father was, are very relevant to the main issue.

The Committee's Meetings

The only groups outside the committee invited to appear before them were the TJMF African-American Advisory Committee and some members of the International Center for Jefferson Studies (both Thomas Jefferson Memorial Foundation entities). While I was pointing out to the joint meeting of the two groups that you could not use something as proof if you did not have reliability of this proof, I was shocked to hear the Thomas Jefferson Memorial Foundation Professor of History at the University of Virginia, Peter Onuf, say (and this is accurate to my best recollection): "We don't need proof. We are historians. We write history the way we want to." It is ironic that Mr. Onuf is the Thomas Jefferson Memorial Professor of History at Mr. Jefferson's University but has been quoted as saying, "Sometimes I hate Thomas Jefferson…" In addition, he wrote a paper entitled "The Scholar's Jefferson" for the *William and Mary Quarterly* in which he used the phrase, "Thomas Jefferson, Monster of Self-Deception" (*William and Mary Quarterly*, Volume L, 1993, pp. 671–699.). Also present at this joint meeting was Jan Lewis who had written an article with Peter Onuf which was published in the January 2000 issue of *William and Mary Quarterly* (and interestingly enough, published almost at the same time as the release of the TJMF Research Committee report in January 2000). This article seemed to go along with some of the other articles in the *Quarterly* denigrating Thomas Jefferson.

When the committee was assembling for one of its meetings in February 1999, the head of the Archaeology Department at Monticello dropped a packet of papers on the table next to me and said (and this is exactly how another member of the committee and I recollect it): "I've got him!" He repeated this statement again and then explained his 'Monte Carlo Simulation.' This just seemed to be an inappropriately enthusiastic remark for someone who is working at Thomas Jefferson's home. When his article was listed in Appendix I of the TJMF Research Committee Report and simultaneously published in the *William and Mary Quarterly* in January 2000, it contained a serious and glaring error that had been pointed out to him. This error was his statement that the "molecular geneticists found the Jefferson Y-haplotype in recognized male-line descendants of **Thomas Jefferson**"! He should have said, **descendants of Field Jefferson, Thomas Jefferson's uncle.** Why the TJMF allowed this significant error to be published in their report and in the *W&M Quarterly* remains unanswered. Future historical researchers will possibly quote this erroneous statement and think that the DNA sample came directly from Thomas Jefferson's direct descendants and that this cinches the case in the Sally Hemings paternity story.

When the DNA Study Committee concluded its meetings in early April 1999 after about two and one half months work, I found that I was right when I reported to Dan Jordan in early March that the committee had reached their decision long before all of the information had been studied, and that sure enough, all of the evidence that would have exonerated Mr. Jefferson had been discarded. I felt compelled to prepare a dissenting report as an attachment, entitled "Minority Report to the

DNA Study Report." On Monday, April 12, 1999, I sent the original signed report to Dianne Swann-Wright, chair of the DNA Study Committee, and personally gave another signed copy to Dan Jordan, President of the TJMF. As it turned out, the chairperson did not acknowledge receiving the report, and I later discovered on January 24, 2000, that she had not shared my dissenting report with the other members of the committee. No discussion of the dissenting report was held with the committee. And as it turned out, the Minority Report was not shared with the interpretive staff at Monticello nor with the Thomas Jefferson Memorial Foundation Board of Trustees until I began to circulate it after the press conference held by the TJMF on January 26, 2000.

Around the second week of January 2000, I was called into Dan Jordan's office and given an advanced copy of the TJMF Research Committee (DNA Study Committee) report and the statement of the TJMF regarding the conclusions. After glancing at the conclusions, I disagreed with the statement of the TJMF.

If the TJMF and the DNA Study Committee majority had been seeking the truth and had used accurate legal and historical information rather than being led by politically correct motivation, their statement should have been something like this: "After almost two hundred years of study including recent DNA information, it is still impossible to prove with absolute certainty whether Thomas Jefferson did or did not father any of Sally Hemings' children." This statement is accurate and honest and it would have helped discourage the campaign by leading universities (including Thomas Jefferson's own University of Virginia), magazines, university publications, national commercial and public TV networks, and newspapers to denigrate and destroy the legacy of one of the greatest of our founding fathers and one of the greatest of all our citizens.

I did not then have time to digest the Research Committee report. As I was preparing to leave his office, Jordan said that he did not want me to give my Minority Report at the time of the TJMF press conference on January 26, 2000. This was the first time that I had heard anything about the Minority Report since I had submitted it nine months before. I did not understand why he would make this request. But I did not know that the report had not been shared with those that should have seen it! I had not even thought about giving the report to the media anyway, because I thought that it would be attached to the Research Committee report and that the media would have access to it. That evening, and after having had time to look through the TJMF report, it became apparent as to why the Minority Report was not to be presented to the media: it was not attached to the Research Committee report! I wrote Dan Jordan and insisted that the Minority Report be attached to the TJMF report. No reply was received. Seventy-two hours before the press release, the DNA Study Committee met with Dan Jordan. After being thanked for the time and effort the committee had given to this project, we were given the final Research Committee report and the TJMF statement and dismissed. As we were leaving the meeting, I asked several of the members of the committee what they thought of the Minority Report. To my surprise, they said that they had never seen it!! Later, I contacted two members of the TJMF Board of Trustees and they said that they also had not been given a copy of the dissenting Minority Report. Strange! They met with me and were given copies of the Minority Report and told of my concern about the entire scenario then taking place at Monticello. Next I was asked to come by Dan Jordan's office, and we had a discussion about these events. I again asked him to attach the Minority Report to the Research Committee report. He refused at that time. I informed him that it was going to look extremely bad for the Foundation if the press realized that they had not been given the dissenting report; that I had been, in effect, gagged by the TJMF; that the Board of Trustees of the Foundation had been denied access to the dissenting report; that the chairperson of the DNA Study Committee had not shared the dissenting report with the other members of the committee, nor allowed discussion of it; and that the interpretative staff also had not been given the Minority Report. He said he would think about this, and one week later he had changed his mind and said that the dissenting report would be shared with all and would become an attachment to the Research Committee report.

The DNA Study Committee had finished its work in early April '99. Lucia (Cinder) Stanton apparently wrote the final report and more than likely finished it by late April or early May 1999. After it was completed, the DNA Study Committee members did not discuss nor even see the final report until 72 hours before its release to the press, and even then there was no discussion of the content or of any changes. *And remember that the report was not released until nine months after completion of the committee's work.* There were also some strange coincidences associated with the timing of the release. For example, several of the members of the committee and its consultants were allowed to publish their work in the *William and Mary Quarterly*, which was also released about the same time as the TJMF report. Martin Luther King's birthday was 9 days before the TJMF media event. Black History month was less than a week after the TJMF timed release. And the despicable CBS miniseries on Thomas Jefferson and Sally Hemings which was politically reconfigured, riddled with falsehoods and alterations of the truth and of history, and denigrating to a Founding Father, was aired about two weeks later. Interestingly, the Thomas Jefferson Memorial Foundation did not rise to the defense of Thomas Jefferson and they discouraged their historical interpreters (i.e., the guides) from making any comments about the miniseries.

Mr. Jordan's invitation to the public to read both reports (DNA Study Committee and Minority Report) and draw their own conclusions has produced an immense positive response to the "Minority Report" from Jefferson scholars, historians, physicians, scientists, statisticians, active and retired college professors, attorneys, genealogists, and the general public. Many of those who have taken the time to read the TJMF report have been shocked to see the evidence that the committee used to reach their conclusions.

The Foundation's response by Ms. Stanton said that the committee as a whole did not feel the Minority Report was of sufficient weight to warrant a different conclusion. This statement is anything but the truth, because the committee as a whole did not see the Minority Report until well after the release of the final committee report on January 27, 2000. In other words, the chair of the committee did not share the dissenting report (which was submitted on April 12, 1999) with the complete committee. As a matter of fact, the committee as a whole did not even see the final DNA Study Committee report until 72 hours prior to the release of this report to the public, and there was no time to discuss the contents at that time (the committee had finished its deliberations in April 1999—nine months earlier).

In conclusion, I have truly tried to record these events as I can remember or document them. I am intensely loyal to Thomas Jefferson and his legacy; but the public and scholars will have to determine the propriety and motivation of this study, and the conclusions about Sally Hemings and Thomas Jefferson reached by the DNA Study Committee and the TJMF. If they had been seeking the truth beyond any reasonable doubt and had not found it, they should have so stated.

A Monticello Guide's Insider View

C. Michael Moffitt, Ph.D.

I worked as a Monticello Associate House Guide/Interpreter for nearly one year, from March 1999 to February 2000. My educational and professional background is in the environmental and biological sciences, having worked in this broad field for approximately 25 years. I have always been a great admirer and student of Thomas Jefferson, with a particular interest in his views and varied activities relating to nature and science. Therefore, I welcomed the opportunity to work for the Thomas Jefferson Memorial Foundation (TJMF) during a time period after I had sold a consulting firm that I had operated for 10 years. My tenure at Monticello was a bittersweet experience—the bitter aspect culminating after the January 26, 2000, public release of the TJMF Research Committee's "Report on Thomas Jefferson and Sally Hemings."

Prior to the release of that report, I (like most of the Monticello guides) made mention during visitors' tours of the DNA study which was reported by Dr. Eugene Foster in a brief article under "Scientific Correspondence" in the November 5, 1998, issue of the journal *Nature*. Although the study certainly did not prove that Thomas Jefferson fathered a child with his slave Sally Hemings, it did appear to indicate that "a" male Jefferson fathered one of the purported children of Hemings—a son named Eston, born in 1808. We know from readily available information that there were at least eight male Jeffersons who potentially visited at Monticello during that period and could have been the father of Eston Hemings. Thomas Jefferson may be the least likely candidate, given he was 64 years old at the time of Eston's estimated conception in an era when the average life span of a man was approximately 45 to 50 years. The study did appear to show, with much more confidence, that *no* male in the Jefferson line fathered Thomas Woodson, whose descendants had a strong oral tradition that he was the son of Thomas Jefferson. Generally, I would relate the facts of the geneticists' study to my tour groups and end the brief overview by stating that no one will likely ever know for sure whether a relationship existed between Thomas Jefferson and Sally Hemings. However, I would also add that nearly all of the eminent Jefferson scholars to date, including Dan Jordan, President of the TJMF, had essentially ruled out the possibility of this relationship. After all, this politically motivated rumor of a liaison, spread first in 1802 by James Thomson Callender, had been dismissed as fictional by Dumas Malone and others years before.

However, my and the other guides' ability to maintain the level of this discussion on a purely factual, scientific basis ended when the TJMF released the Research Committee's report. Suddenly the foundation I worked for, whose primary role is the factual interpretation of Thomas Jefferson's life and the preservation of his home, was telling the world with this report, according to Daniel P. Jordan, Ph.D., President, that there is a "strong likelihood that Thomas Jefferson and Sally Hemings had a relationship over time that led to the birth of one, and perhaps all, of the known children of Sally Hemings." Compare this statement by Dr. Jordan with his feelings on this same issue a few years ago. In an interview for Ken Burns' 1996 film "Thomas Jefferson," Dan Jordan was asked if Sally Hemings was Thomas Jefferson's mistress. Dr. Jordan answered, "There's no historical evidence that there was a relationship between Thomas Jefferson and Sally. She enters the scene as a 14-year-old in France, where she had come along somewhat unexpectedly to accompany Jefferson's youngest daughter. There are oral traditions that are in conflict. There are many blacks today who believe they are descendants of that possible union. On the other hand, there's another oral tradition that would say that the paternity rested with others than Thomas Jefferson. *My own belief is that, as one of the contemporaries of Jefferson said, it would be morally impossible for that relationship to have occurred."* (emphasis added) Dr. Jordan went on to say that Jefferson "was totally devoted to his family and he had 11 grandchildren living with him. And one of the granddaughters lived essentially directly above him. She heard everything. She heard him when he got up in the morning and sang Scottish airs and the like. . . . There are no secrets on a plantation, certainly not at Monticello. And his family, to whom he was totally devoted, completely discounted this possibility." (The Jordan interview can be found on the PBS web site at www.pbs.org/jefferson/archives/interviews/Jordan.htm.)

What could have so dramatically altered Dr. Jordan's opinion on this issue in the last four to five years after a lifetime of study of Jefferson? Certainly there was no additional historical evidence uncovered during this period. The only new piece of information was the brief, non-peer reviewed publication of a DNA study that linked *some* male Jefferson to one child of Sally Hemings, and completely ruled out Jefferson's paternity for another purported child. No other genetic information was even available from descendants of the other purported children of Sally Hemings. Surely, this wasn't enough to change Dr. Jordan's strong earlier beliefs and the entire interpretation of Jefferson's life at his home, Monticello! Yet, after the Research Committee's report was released in January 2000, the house guides were told to always speak of the report during their tours and to echo its conclusions. In fact, a series of "training" sessions were required of the house guides to insure that they would incorporate information from the report into their house tours.

The Monticello house guides first received a copy of the Research Committee's report on the day it was released to the media and the public. In fact, it was handed out to the guides who attended a TJMF staff meeting *after* it had been distributed to the press and Dr. Jordan had already held his press conference. Even the two guides who were members of the Research Committee did not receive copies of the report until

72 hours prior to release, and neither was asked to help write it. What I wasn't aware of at the time was that Dr. Ken Wallenborn, one of the guides who was a full member of the Committee, had written a dissenting minority opinion to the Committee's report nine months earlier, but that report was suppressed. It had not been given to other committee members, it was not released to the press, and it was not mentioned at the guides staff meeting by Dr. Jordan or Dianne Swann-Wright, Chair of the Research Committee.

My first impression of the Research Committee's report after reviewing it thoroughly was that it must have been meant as an in-house compilation of *some* of the information relating to the Jefferson-Hemings issue—in essence, a work-in-progress. I hadn't been deeply researching the issue at this point, but it was quickly evident to me that some very pertinent information that I had previously heard of, but which would conflict with the Report's official conclusion, had been excluded or dismissed by the committee. It appeared that the 1802 stories written by the discredited James Callender were being taken as serious "evidence" of Jefferson's relationship with Sally Hemings, yet other writings of his that were exculpatory to Jefferson were apparently overlooked. Further, the Hemings family oral histories were being treated as indisputable facts, whereas Jefferson family or friends' statements were dismissed as highly suspect. The report was obviously biased, but not having been a member of the Committee itself, I was not aware of how this came to pass.

I tendered my resignation to the TJMF on February 23, 2000, approximately one month after the release of the Committee's report. In my resignation letter, I related my concerns regarding the very biased (in my opinion) Research Committee report and the procedures the Committee had followed that led up to the release of the report to the press. Further, I expressed my great concerns that Dr. Wallenborn's minority report had not been attached to the TJMF's report, particularly since he was such an important member of the Committee that Dr. Jordan had singled him out for mention in his statement which preceded the report. Dr. Jordan wrote, "Shortly thereafter, I appointed a staff research committee that included four Ph.D.'s (one with advanced study in genetics) and an M.D." Nowhere in Dr. Jordan's January 26, 2000, statement does he mention that this particular M.D. disagreed with the report's conclusion and had submitted a minority opinion.

The third area that I mentioned as a grave concern in my resignation letter was the situation surrounding the timing of the release of the Committee report. Nine months passed after the Committee finished its meetings before the report was released. Yet, the decision to finally release it to the public occurred one week before the beginning of Black History month, and approximately two weeks before the airing of the fantastic and absurd CBS mini-series on Thomas Jefferson and Sally Hemings called "Sally Hemings: An American Scandal." It seemed likely that the coincidence of these events gave undeserved credibility to, and additional advanced publicity for, the television production. CBS probably could not have purchased the amount of publicity it received by the timing of this controversial report somehow "confirming" a long-term and child-bearing relationship between the two figures. It was not until later I heard that, apparently, Dianne Swann-Wright and Lucia Stanton of the Research Committee had visited the mini-series set during filming and had also attended the film's premier screening with a number of the members of the Hemings and Woodson family descendants.

I was disappointed that the TJMF, whose foremost duty surely is public education and the dissemination of truth related to Thomas Jefferson and his life, had issued no criticism of the specific portions of this television production which distorted and intentionally altered well-documented facts and events in the life of Thomas Jefferson. Jefferson's letters, conversations, details of his death, and even his plantation buildings were significantly altered to somehow fictionally associate them with the Sally Hemings character. The Monticello house guides suddenly began to get fantastic questions from visitors (many of whom believed the mini-series had actually been filmed at Monticello) such as, "Where's the room (or house) that Jefferson built for Sally?" At the same time, my house guide supervisor told me that the guides were not to say anything critical of the CBS production during their tours.

My greatest concern regarding this whole issue is that individuals today who wish to attack and denigrate one of the greatest of our founding fathers, Thomas Jefferson, seem to think they have found a license to do so in the TJMF's report and conclusion. Jefferson has been called everything from a child molester to a slave-raping monster in the press, and almost every such story cites the findings of the Research Committee's report to add credibility or validity to this hideous and unfounded claim. I shudder to think of the impression that this entire ugly process has left on our nation's children.

Research Report on the Jefferson-Hemings Controversy: A Critical Analysis

Eyler Robert Coates, Sr.

On January 26, 2000, the Thomas Jefferson Memorial Foundation announced that it had reached a conclusion concerning the Jefferson-Hemings controversy. Their basic finding was that there is "a high probability that Thomas Jefferson fathered Eston Hemings, and that he most likely was the father of all six of Sally Hemings' children." However, an examination of this report and the methodology used in preparing it shows it to be an unprofessional, unscientific accumulation of bias and prejudice, and an offense to the memory of the great man that this foundation was chartered to memorialize.

One would expect the Foundation at least to give Thomas Jefferson the benefit of the doubt in the face of the many scurrilous attacks that have been made on his character over the years, for which there is not one shred of direct evidence. But as we shall demonstrate below, the exact opposite is the case. The best evidence was suppressed or ignored, competent persons having opposing views were not consulted, and many alternative but reasonable explanations for the circumstantial evidence were disregarded. As the reader of this analysis will clearly see, it is obvious that the entire controversy was not approached, as advertised (and as Jefferson had written), "to follow truth wherever it may lead." Rather, there was a deliberate attempt to select and mold the evidence to fit a pre-selected theory and to avoid anything that might resemble genuine balance. The results and conclusions became precise illustrations of something that Jefferson had written on a different occasion:

> "The moment a person forms a theory, his imagination sees, in every object, only the traits which favor that theory."

> —Thomas Jefferson to Charles Thompson, 1787.

This travesty of a report sees in every point only those aspects that favor the preconceived theory. It leaves unconsidered much evidence that would tend to exonerate Jefferson, and it avoids connecting different pieces of evidence that would point away from Thomas Jefferson to some other member of his family or household.

The basic failure of the report derives from there being no rational and reasonable basis for evaluating evidence. Certainly, the report contains no statement of the committee's policy in that regard. But by examining the decisions that were made when interpreting evidence, it is possible to determine what appears to be the subjective grounds on which the committee made such decisions. Rather than giving emphasis to evidence based on the apparent ability of the testifier to know of his or her own knowledge and experience whether the evidence was true or not, the committee judged evidence on the same basis established by Annette Gordon-Reed in her book, *Thomas Jefferson and Sally Hemings: An American Controversy* (GR p. 103), in which she wrote that "the standard for judging the evidence... should be what the declarants say, how they say it, and the amount of extrinsic evidence that exists to support their statements." And since the "extrinsic evidence" is all based on conjecture and supposition, following that standard means the entire operation becomes a subjective one over which the investigator's bias, either consciously or unconsciously, has complete sway. The result is a fabricated tissue of hearsay and assumptions, in which gossip and self-serving, handed-down family stories are granted the equivalence of facts and direct testimony. Even the report's so-called "uncontested historical facts" are so lacking in close and insightful analysis, they become mere tools for the investigators' bias. The only exception to this incompetent, unprofessional approach to evidence evaluation is the uninterpreted DNA test results, which by their very nature cannot be manipulated.

The chief error committed by the committee was in equating oral tradition—another name for handed-down hearsay—to solid evidence. As David Rafner of Richmond, Va., wrote in USA Today Online, Feb. 1, 2000, "Hearsay is hearsay, no matter how many generations it has been repeated. It can spur investigations but can never be raised to the status of evidence." Or perhaps "*should* never be raised" to that status, because that is precisely what the committee has done. Vague standards of evidence, such as those the committee employed, permit the introduction of data from unknown and unverifiable sources, which is what family tradition is. And as we shall see, with the Woodson family tradition, we now have *scientific proof* that even the strongest oral tradition can be absolutely false, especially on the question of paternity.

The evidence of paternity is one kind of evidence that surfaces in several different contexts and that deserves to be singled out for special attention. In the absence of DNA testing, *it is all but impossible for third parties to know with certainty if a given man is the father of a woman's child.* Often, not even the man himself can know this, and sometimes even the woman cannot be sure, especially if she has had several different sexual partners in a short period of time. In the case of an unmarried woman, living on a plantation that has dozens of potential sexual partners also living there, and that is visited by hundreds of visitors in any given year, no person can be certain who might be the father of any child that the woman has. Third parties can only guess, based on whatever information might be available to them or observations they may have made.

In considering whether there was a relationship between Thomas Jefferson and Sally Hemings, we shall be compelled to consider evidence from a variety of sources, most of whom could not possibly have an inkling (based on their own knowledge) as to whether there was such a relationship or not. But this apparently does not keep them from offering testimony. Some make assertions about the paternity of children that were conceived before the testifier was even born! Others not living on the plantation make assertions but supply no reason or event that would substantiate their assertion, thus making their story pure unsupported opinion and gossip. For others, though their observations may be true, they may mistakenly read into them more than is there. Therefore, in considering all the testimony that has been given, whenever anyone states the exact identity of a person said to be the father of a child, we must keep in mind that it is virtually impossible for them to assert this with absolute certainty, and we must evaluate what they say on the basis of how probable it is that they themselves observed what they are reporting and how likely it was that their interpretation of what they saw was valid.

Historical and Scientific Facts

The Research Findings of the Foundation's report may be divided into two parts: (1) a series of nine "historical and scientific facts" which the committee considered "uncontested," and (2) the interpretation of those facts in the form of commentary under each of the nine headings. Three of the so-called "uncontested facts" are easily acknowledged to be true, since they are based on rigorous scientific fact. A couple of the "historical facts" are not very significant even if true, a couple are based on plain gossip and conjecture, and a couple are not entirely accurate, and therefore are actually contestable on that account. There are several historical facts that would tend to contradict the committee's preformed theory and, therefore, undermine the resulting conclusions of the Research Findings. But these facts were deliberately omitted from the list of nine findings, though most were mentioned and briefly discussed and then dismissed somewhere in the report. But where the gross transgressions made by this report occur is in the interpretations which the committee included under each "uncontested" fact. We will briefly note first the so-called "uncontested facts," followed by the facts that were *not* given full consideration, and then that will be followed by an examination of the interpretations given by the report to the "uncontested facts."

Scientific facts. The fact that there was a DNA match between a single descendant of Eston Hemings and the descendants of Field Jefferson, and the fact that there was *no* match between the descendants of John Carr and the descendant of Eston Hemings, together with the fact that

78

there was *no* match between the descendants of Tom Woodson and Field Jefferson, are all scientific facts that are without question indisputable. They are straightforward and not subject to interpretive manipulation of the scientific findings themselves. In fact, they stand as solid benchmarks, requiring that all other circumstantial evidence not transgress the facts they establish. It is only when elements of gossip, unreliable historical data, and imaginative manipulations of the reliable data are added to these scientific facts that distorted conclusions are reached.

Insignificant facts. The fact that the descendants of Madison Hemings passed down the story that they were descended from Thomas Jefferson and Sally Hemings, and the fact that Eston and possibly other of Sally's children were said to resemble Jefferson are both facts of no great significance. The Woodson descendants also passed down a similar story, and the DNA evidence proved they were mistaken. Monticello was swarming with Jefferson's relatives from time to time, and any of them could have been the father of Sally's children, thus providing the "resemblance" to Thomas Jefferson.

Gossip and hearsay. The fact that several persons not in Jefferson's actual household believed that Thomas Jefferson was the father of Sally's children, together with the fact that Madison Hemings told a newspaper reporter the same things, is not *evidence* but hearsay and gossip.

Uncontested facts? More uncertain as "uncontested facts" are the assertions that Sally's birth patterns match Thomas Jefferson's presence at Monticello, and that Sally's children were granted a unique access to freedom. Both of these "facts" are not as clearly established as has been assumed. The birth patterns raise several questions. There were many times when Jefferson was present and Sally could have become pregnant but did not. And the access to freedom has a simple and obvious explanation, which will be explained in detail below.

The overriding point that must be recognized with each one of these nine "scientific and historical facts" is, not a single one of them is solid, direct evidence that there was a relationship between Sally Hemings and Thomas Jefferson. All taken together, they are not cumulative, and do not suggest that one piece added to another produces a convincing combination or a series of steps moving in the same direction. For example, if

Sally's child conceived in France had the Jefferson Y chromosome, and Thomas Jefferson was the only Jefferson there, then that combination of evidence would indicate that Thomas was the father. But if a child of Sally's had the Jefferson Y chromosome and there were any number of Jeffersons around to impregnate her, then those two facts would not combine to point to Thomas; they are just isolated facts.

Rather than resulting in such combinations, all the above "scientific and historical facts" are just unrelated observations subject to multiple explanations, or they are gossip and hearsay that have no explanation to back them up. In fact, the best kinds of evidence tend to exonerate Thomas Jefferson, but that evidence was overlooked or dismissed for insubstantial reasons and omitted as part of the nine major points!

Omitted Facts

One of the interesting aspects of this Research Report, presented to the public as a fair and even-handed consideration of the question of Thomas Jefferson's paternity of Sally Hemings' children, is that there are no facts presented and considered in the Findings as items that would tend to exonerate Jefferson. That alone suggests that this was a put-up job, intended not to provide a careful analysis and consideration of *all* the facts, but a one-sided argument in pursuit of political ends, a piece of propaganda intended to persuade and promote a particular idea. That this kind of polemic would issue forth from a foundation established to memorialize Thomas Jefferson is itself one of the incredible ironies of this whole story. The Foundation itself engaged in a sorry attempt to defame one of our great founding fathers.

Nevertheless, we will attempt to remedy this oversight, and present a few salient facts that the Foundation might have included in their list, were they inclined to present a balanced report. Perhaps the Foundation thought that these facts are "contested," and therefore not proper for consideration. Not so! These are actual historical facts. The fact that they occurred cannot be contested. The contestation comes, not as to whether they actually occurred or not, but on the *interpretation* given to these facts. And since the Foundation presented its own interpretations of the "uncontested historical or scientific facts," one would think that they would at least present these historical facts, and then try to tear them down through interpretation, if that was thought necessary.

Moreover, as we have seen, some of the "uncontested" facts which the Foundation *did* present can indeed be contested. But it appears the Foundation did not feel compelled to provide equal consideration to facts that might tend to exonerate Jefferson as they did to those which indicted him. Instead, each of these exonerating facts was mentioned off-handedly in relation to other discussions, and dismissed without any serious consideration of the pros and cons. What is fascinating here is the trivial reasons the committee gives for dismissing some of the most important pieces of evidence available relating to the supposed relationship between Sally Hemings and Thomas Jefferson. Also interesting is the arbitrary manner the committee adopted in evaluating evidence, narrowing or broadening their criteria, depending on whether the evidence supported their theory of the relationship or not.

Jefferson's denial in his letter to Secretary Smith. The assertion that Jefferson never denied these charges is not entirely true. He thought that to make public denials only draws attention to the attacker:

> "I should have fancied myself half guilty, had I condescended to
> put pen to paper in refutation of their falsehoods, or drawn
> them respect by any notice from myself."

—Thomas Jefferson to George Logan, June 20, 1816.

That passage includes an implied denial, since Jefferson is suggesting that only those who are guilty become concerned with obviously unscrupulous attacks. And while it is true that Jefferson never denied such accusations *publicly*, he did deny them in private correspondence. The historical record provides a reference to a denial letter, but the denial letter itself has been lost or destroyed. In a private cover letter to his Secretary of the Navy, Robert Smith (covering a copy of a letter of denial to his Attorney General, Levi Lincoln), he denied all the accusations made against him, except for the singular one related to a Mrs. Walker. This was well after the accusations by Callender, and he wrote:

> "You will perceive that I plead guilty to one of their charges,
> that when young and single I offered love to a handsome lady. I

acknowledge its incorrectness. It is the only one founded in
truth among all their allegations against me."

—Thomas Jefferson to Robert Smith, July 1, 1805.

That response should leave no doubt whatever that he was denying *all*
the allegations, including the rumors and charges that he had children by
any of his slaves. Nevertheless, some proponents of an affair have suggested that Jefferson was being coy, and that "all their allegations"
referred only to the allegations made by Mr. Walker. Walker's allegations
"might not have" included allegations that Jefferson fathered children by
a slave, which was one of the allegations made by his other enemies. But
the fact is, as the report's own findings indicate, this was one of several
letters that Jefferson wrote "to some close political associates" in response
to the "assaults on his character" made by Federalist newspapers, and that
is the context in which Jefferson made his denial. It is this kind of twist-
ing of the evidence with imputations of connivance on the part of
Jefferson which is typical of the manipulations made by affair proponents. Nevertheless, lest there be any remaining doubt, it should be
noted that not too long after writing the letter to Smith, Jefferson also
wrote:

"There is not a truth on earth which I fear or would disguise.
But secret slanders cannot be disarmed, because they are secret."

—Thomas Jefferson to William Duane, March 22, 1806.

And a few months before he died, Jefferson wrote the following:

"There is not a truth existing which I fear or would wish
unknown to the whole world."

—Thomas Jefferson to Henry Lee, May 15, 1826.

Of course, never-say-die proponents will probably come back and say
that this last quote must be taken in context, and refers only to political
subjects, in spite of the fact that Jefferson plainly wrote, "not a truth
existing." But as Jefferson said, when a person clings to a theory, he sees
only the things that favor that theory. And, we might add, he twists
everything else he sees so that it supports that theory.

Martha Jefferson Randolph's confrontation with Thomas Jefferson. There is one story included in the Foundation's report that provides good behavioristic evidence that also contradicts the report's findings. The report states, "There is only one known account of the subject [i.e., a connection to Sally Hemings] being raised in Jefferson's presence. As Jefferson's Randolph granddaughters told biographer Henry S. Randall, Jefferson's daughter Martha Randolph, roused to indignation by Irish poet Thomas Moore's couplet linking her father with a slave, thrust the offending poem in front of him one day at Monticello. Jefferson's only response was a 'hearty, clear laugh.' "

Proponents of an affair say that Martha knew what was going on, but she was "in denial." That is nonsense. If she were really in denial, she would hardly have angrily presented the poem to Jefferson. Instead, reality would have clashed with her hidden refusal to accept it, and she would more likely have angrily thrown the poem in the trash and blotted it from her mind. What she did was not denial, but *confrontation*. And having presented the poem to Jefferson, if he were really guilty, he would surely not have responded with a hearty, clear laugh (unless he had the character of Al Capone, which he obviously did not), but would have blanched at having his private affairs publicly ridiculed and especially being faced with it directly by his own beloved daughter. But instead he laughed, and his laughing indicates to any reasonable person that he thought the whole thing utterly absurd. Rather than indicating that there was an affair, and that Jefferson and his daughter both refused to face up to it, this incident clearly indicates to anyone with a sensitivity to human nature that neither Jefferson nor his daughter really believed with any part of their minds that this story was true.

Martha Jefferson Randolph's denial on her deathbed. Shortly before her death, Martha called her two sons, Thomas Jefferson Randolph and George Wythe Randolph, to her bedside and told them of Mr. Jefferson's innocence of the charges of fathering children by a female slave, citing her reasons, and asking them always to defend the character of their illustrious grandfather. One of the important things to recognize here is that Martha herself *thought* that Thomas Jefferson was not the father of Sally's children, and since she had lived at Monticello much of the time when Jefferson was there, and was on the closest terms with him, she was in a position to know from her own knowledge and observation whether there was likely a relationship going on or not. Certainly, she was in a better position to do this than someone like Israel Jefferson (see below), who was a child, ran errands, and had only very limited contact with Jefferson. She may have been mistaken as to *who* the father of Sally's children actually was (and then she may not have been with respect to some of the children). But she either sincerely believed Jefferson was not the father, or she was lying through her teeth on her death bed. Fictional accounts of the supposed "affair" are invariably compelled to portray Martha as knowing about it fully, because that is the only thing that makes sense if indeed there was an affair. She was there, and could hardly have missed it, if it did occur. But all the real evidence indicates that Martha did not believe it.

Edmund Bacon's eyewitness account and denial. Edmund Bacon reported seeing someone other than Thomas Jefferson coming from Sally's room early in the morning, and offered that as evidence that Jefferson was not the father of Harriet. Bacon was an overseer for Thomas Jefferson, and related the following story about his employer:

> "He freed one girl some years before he died, and there was a great deal of talk about it. She was nearly as white as anybody, and very beautiful. People said he freed her because she was his own daughter. She was not his daughter; she was _____'s daughter. I know that. I have seen him come out of her mother's room many a morning, when I went up to Monticello very early." (JB p. 102)

The report dismisses this account because Bacon supposedly was not working for Jefferson at the time Harriet was conceived, and therefore it is assumed that he could not have known who Harriet's father was. But it doesn't take much insight to understand what Bacon was saying, even if he was not working at Monticello before Harriet was conceived. Just as the committee assumes that Sally's children did not have multiple fathers, Bacon was no doubt assuming that whoever he saw coming out of Sally's room was Sally's longtime lover, and therefore the father of Harriet. In any case, what Bacon was saying was that Thomas Jefferson was *not* the father of Sally's children, because he—Bacon—was an eyewitness to the fact that someone else—*not* Thomas Jefferson—was sleeping with Sally. The committee assumes Sally to be "monogamous" with respect to Thomas Jefferson, but apparently cannot consider that she might have been assumed to be "monogamous" when considering Edmund Bacon's evidence. Here is another example of how the committee deals with evidence that they don't want to accept: they become very strict, and narrow the focus so that if Bacon's account is not a perfect fit, it gets thrown out. When they consider something like the Cocke diary (see below), they can broaden the focus and consider his diary as evidence, even though Cocke had no stated reason whatsoever to back up the accusations he made.

Nevertheless, Bacon's account is one of the most important pieces of evidence in existence bearing on a relationship between Sally Hemings and Thomas Jefferson. *Bacon was the only observer to express an opinion on Jefferson's paternity and then back it up with eyewitness evidence!* Every other piece of so-called evidence that identifies Thomas Jefferson as the father of Sally's children is gossip, hearsay, conjecture, or supposition, and provides no reasons or firsthand evidence to back up the statements that are made. In fact, most of it doesn't even cite the source or give any indication how the source might have known what it asserts! It is easy to understand why a biased committee would want to dismiss this evidence with a simple "has problems of chronology."

The fact that the name of the person Bacon identified was later scratched out would tend to suggest that someone was trying to hide the truth or protect the identity of the true perpetrator. We could only speculate on who that perpetrator might be. The essential point for our needs here, however, is that it was *not* Thomas Jefferson.

The confession of Peter Carr. One of the more startling omissions in the committee's report is the absence of any serious consideration given to the confessions by Peter Carr. In a criminal trial, if there exists a confession by a perpetrator, that alone can determine the outcome of the trial. Yet in the case of who was sleeping with Sally, evidence of a confession is completely brushed aside. There are several reasons why this crucial information was disregarded, of course, but none of them are valid.

There are two stories regarding the Carr brothers and the alleged fathering of Sally's children by Peter Carr. In one of the two stories, historian Henry S. Randall relates that Thomas Jefferson Randolph told him of the Carr brothers crying when Randolph confronted them with a newspaper article accusing Thomas Jefferson of fathering mulatto children. They wept because, as they reportedly said, their uncle was being disgraced for something that was their own doing. In another story, Ellen Randolph Coolidge wrote that T. J. Randolph had told her that he had overheard Peter Carr laughing, and telling a friend that "the old gentleman had to bear the blame of his and Sam's misdeed." Proponents of an affair note a big difference between the two stories, and suggest for that reason that the stories are made-up and not true. But that is foolish and undiscerning. Nothing about the difference in the two stories suggests that they can't both be true. The circumstances were entirely different for each, and that would easily account for the different reactions. Aren't we all familiar with the man who will laugh and tell dirty jokes to his friends, but is embarrassed to do so before the minister of his church? There is nothing uncommon about such duplicitous behavior, and the fact that biased persons want to disregard the confessions on that basis only means that they will grab at any grounds, however insubstantial they may be, to eliminate evidence that undermines the case they are trying to make.

The other reason for dismissing the Carr confession is that it was demonstrated wrong in the case of the father of Eston, since the DNA evidence demonstrates decisively that it was a Jefferson, not a Carr, that was Eston's father. Here again, biased investigators are trying first to suggest that Sally had all her children by one male—something for which there is no evidence whatsoever—and then having made that assumption, they try to say that the DNA test proves that neither of the Carr brothers was that male. But this is fallacious thinking. Even though the DNA tests demonstrate conclusively that *some* Jefferson was the father of Eston Hemings, that in no way excludes the possibility that one of the Carr brothers was father of some of Sally's other children. Until DNA tests can be conducted on the descendants of Sally's other children, the Carr brothers are still prime suspects as father for her children other than Eston, since there is evidence for this which on its face is highly compelling. This is not mere gossip or other kinds of guess-work, but evidence of actual confessions overheard and related by Thomas Jefferson's grandson. And a confession, like eyewitness testimony, is one of the strongest kinds of evidence that is available to us. Only the most biased and incompetent investigator would dismiss such evidence on such flimsy grounds, and accept in its place gossip and hearsay.

The interesting thing regarding the possibility that Sally's children had multiple fathers is the way affair proponents are avoiding any further testing of Hemings descendants. After seventeen months of search, Herbert Barger, a Jefferson family historian and genealogist, was able to locate the body of William Hemings, son of Madison Hemings, whose grave site was long-forgotten by other Hemings family members. William died in 1910, and it is highly possible that usable DNA can be taken from his burial site. The information gained from this testing would be infinitely more valuable than Dr. Eugene Foster's testing of yet another of the Woodson descendants (see below). It should be borne in mind that there was only *one single line of descent* from Eston that was tested. That single line is the *only* scientific link between the Hemings and the Jeffersons. Nevertheless Dr. Foster, Dan Jordan, president of the Foundation, and now the living relatives of William Hemings, all express no particular interest in having these tests made on William Hemings. In fact, the relatives are adamantly opposed. Dan Jordan says he doesn't think the family should be "pressured." The family at first gave their oral consent, but then have refused to sign a written document to permit the exhumation. But as someone remarked recently, if we have no qualms about digging up a former President to see if he died from cherry jubilee, why should this be a problem?

So why this profound lack of interest? Why wouldn't these people, who say they are so interested in following truth "wherever it may lead," want to pursue this possibility for adding more scientific knowledge to help settle this controversy? The reason is obvious, because if those tests showed someone other than a Jefferson to be the father—perhaps even a Carr!—then that would blow this whole Jefferson-Hemings Relationship Theory to smithereens. Of course, if the tests showed a match to the Jefferson Y chromosome, that would not seal the case on Thomas Jefferson, but it would surely make it a little stronger. But none of these assassins of Thomas Jefferson's reputation want to take that risk. They are not interested in adding some scientific knowledge to the problem, with the chance of vindicating Thomas Jefferson. They are only interested in indicting Thomas Jefferson. They would rather hold on to the gains they think they have now than take the risk of having the whole side-show sent down the tubes. It is interesting to note also that the Research Report mentions that "the committee is aware that further DNA testing [of another Woodson descendant], coordinated by Dr. Foster, is in progress." They bother to note that utterly futile attempt to make Jefferson guilty, but they don't even mention this potentially explosive DNA testing that Herb Barger is trying to promote. So much for the Foundation's commitment to "follow truth wherever it may lead."

It is interesting at this point to note that in order for proponents of an affair to dismiss all the above firsthand evidence, and to substitute in its place the hearsay and gossip that constitutes most of the "historical evidence" which proponents treat as authentic, it is necessary to consider all the above solid, firsthand narratives as coming from people who, for one reason or another, all lied. To proponents, it was all a vast Jefferson family conspiracy. And any error about paternity, which, as we have stipulated, is an extremely difficult fact to ascertain, is cited as sufficient cause for dismissing everything the person had to relate. But we should realize that such a tactic is silly. A person can be wrong about precisely who the father is, but yet be right about other related elements. Paternity is something that only DNA testing can tell us with certainty.

The Woodson family tradition. The Woodson family story is the strongest oral tradition associated with this controversy. If Tom (Hemings) Woodson left Monticello at age twelve, he was old enough to know *of his own knowledge* who his mother was and where he was living before he went to stay with the Woodsons. As with all oral tradition, we cannot accept all of it indiscriminately. It must be carefully evaluated, and one of the bases of evaluation is what Tom Woodson himself could have known, and what he could not have known firsthand. What he could not have known firsthand was the name of the person who was his father, and that is the precise bit of information the DNA tests demonstrate the Woodsons were mistaken about.

The Woodson family tradition poses problems for the theory which the Research Report adopts, and the committee's way of dealing with this is to throw it in the bin labeled 'things that will probably never be completely understood.' But when one realizes that Thomas Jefferson was *not* the father of any of Sally's children, then the Woodson family tradition fits neatly into place. There is no problem dealing with it. Thus we have this situation: the researchers could not make the Woodson oral tradition fit into their theory, especially since the DNA indicates no Jefferson was the father of Tom Woodson. So, what to do? The answer is simple, if Sally is the mother and Jefferson is *not* the father. But that wouldn't fit the theory. So, the committee just pushes it aside, in hopes, no doubt, that the Woodsons would just go away. This does pose some problems for a "38-year affair" and all the accusations by Callender. But, the only solution the committee has is to call it a mystery.

In any case, the Woodson family tradition tells us two things loud and clear: (1) Whether Tom Woodson was Sally's first child or not, there is no question whatsoever that Thomas Jefferson was *not* his father, and (2) whether Tom Woodson was Sally's first child or not, we have a perfect, scientifically-proven example of how utterly worthless even the strongest family oral tradition can be on matters of paternity.

We must remember that the fact that Tom Woodson was *not* a son of any Jefferson male was much more firmly established by the DNA evidence than the supposed paternal relationship between Thomas Jefferson and Eston Hemings. Eston's father was proven to be any one of 25 Jeffersons, which still admits of a large number of *possible* men as the father, with about eight as more likely. But Tom Woodson's father was proven to be from *none* of the Jefferson males living at that time, which positively and absolutely *excludes* each and every individual Jefferson, including Thomas.

It is interesting to note that the Woodson family tradition is so strong, the family itself refuses to accept the results of the DNA tests. Those tests were performed on *five* lines of descent. The living persons tested were all descended from two sons of Tom Woodson, who were born twelve years apart. In order for the DNA tests to be invalid and for Thomas Jefferson to have been Woodson's father, those two sons of Tom Woodson would need to have been fathered illegitimately by the same man, twelve years apart! That is an absurdly unlikely possibility.

In what seems like a pointless and hopelessly futile effort to somehow secure a match with the Field Jefferson descendants, Dr. Foster went to the trouble of testing yet another line of descent from Tom Woodson. Such indefatigable efforts in the face of such absurd odds can only be taken as a measure of the insistence of affair proponents to prove that Thomas Jefferson was the father of Sally's children. Foster did this because *if* Tom Woodson was Sally's Paris-conceived son and could be shown to have the Jefferson Y chromosome, it would then be certain that Thomas Jefferson was his father, since Thomas was the only Jefferson in Paris at the time who could have impregnated Sally. One thing the DNA result does demonstrate, however, is that whoever Tom Woodson's father was, his Y chromosome was one common amongst European whites, not sub-Saharan blacks, and if Tom was Sally's first child, his father was almost surely someone she met in France. Nevertheless, if somehow Dr. Foster had been able to get the results he was seeking with this sixth Woodson descendant, those results would call into question Dr. Foster's whole study, because if there was anything that was proved almost irrefutably and unquestionably by the previous results he had obtained, it is that the Woodson DNA, as previously certified, can be traced all the way back to Tom Woodson himself. This fact makes us wonder whether Dr. Foster himself really understands the science of the DNA testing and the results obtained thus far. The results of the test have been returned, however, and Dr. Foster was terribly disappointed. The match was negative; yet another test has demonstrated that the Woodson family tradition is unquestionably false.

Randolph Jefferson's presence when Eston was conceived. Randolph was invited by Thomas to come to Monticello to visit him and Randolph's twin sister, who had just arrived one day earlier. In a letter dated August 12, 1807, slightly more than nine months prior to Eston's birth on May 21, 1808, Thomas Jefferson wrote his brother Randolph, advising "Our sister Marks [Randolph's twin sister, Mrs. Hastings Marks] arrived here last night and we shall be happy to see you also." (BM p. 21) This twin sister was at Monticello at the time of the writing, and this suggests that Randolph, probably with some of his sons, would not likely delay the journey to see his sister in order to arrive before she departed from her visit. Since the trip to Monticello from Randolph's home could easily be done in less than a day, that would almost certainly put Randolph at Monticello at the correct time to be the father of Eston. And since Randolph had the same Y chromosome as all the other Jefferson males, he would be completely capable of supplying that chromosome to Sally's son, Eston. Any child of Randolph would also likely have the same physical attributes as Thomas. Nevertheless, the committee report rejects the possibility that Randolph was at Monticello at the time Eston was conceived, which we will examine in greater detail below.

Interpretations

The committee's "Research Findings and Implications" are a study in bias. Instead of presenting all the various contradictory interpretations in their best possible light, weighing them against one another, and then providing reasons for choosing the one that is most likely true, the committee presented its findings as conclusions, and dismissed opposing possibilities, evidence, and interpretations out of hand. We examine below the interpretations given under each one of the nine "uncontested historical or scientific facts."

1. DNA match between descendants of Eston Hemings and Field Jefferson. The report says that this match "provides scientific support for the statements of Madison Hemings and Israel Jefferson." But this is a gross overstatement. Both Madison and Israel made numerous and extensive statements completely unrelated to the DNA match. At most, it can only be said that the statements by Madison and Israel that Thomas Jefferson was the father of Sally's children were not contradicted by the DNA match. But there are many other possible explanations that are also not contradicted by this match. The committee's exaggeration, however, illustrates their bias. They also acknowledge the "scientific possibility" that Randolph Jefferson or one of his sons could have been the father. Notice they do not say "provides scientific support," although science supports that possibility just as much as it does the Madison version. But the committee adds, "the preponderance of known historical evidence indicates that Thomas Jefferson was his father." That "preponderance" is presumably presented somewhere else, because it is only stated here as a conclusion. But when we examine that "preponderance" of evidence elsewhere, we find that it is the familiar mix of gossip, hearsay, and speculation. It is a preponderance because the committee chooses to dismiss all the other evidence that contradicts it.

The report then states that "Randolph Jefferson and his sons are not known to have been at Monticello at the time of Eston Hemings' conception." But that statement is false! As we mentioned above, Randolph was invited to come to Monticello to visit with his twin sister at the very time that Sally conceived Eston. It is true, of course, that this letter is the only record of Randolph's probable presence at the time of conception. Nevertheless, the Foundation's report dismisses the possibility of Randolph's presence because "A search of visitors' accounts, memorandum books, and Jefferson's published and unpublished correspondence provided no indication that Randolph did, in fact, come at this time." But there is not likely to be any other record of Randolph's presence except as incidental notes in correspondence just like the note inviting him. The real question is, were there notations in visitors' accounts, and memorandum books indicating all family visits? Were all these visits in fact formally recorded? Would we, for example, know that Randolph's twin sister had come for a visit to Monticello if it had not been mentioned in a letter to Randolph, or possibly in previous correspondence with the sister herself? Was there a formal register that listed casual visits by near relatives? Was the sister's visit recorded? Apparently not. In other words, it is highly likely that such notations were not made except incidental to some important activity or incidentally in correspondence.

To dismiss the possibility of a visit because there was no particular reason for writing about it becomes merely a device to eliminate evidence that is not wanted because it muddies the water. The research report states in Appendix J that existing correspondence between Thomas and Randolph from the year 1807 suggests that similar invitations may have been extended previously, but Randolph "may not always have acted on these invitations. In his post-1807 letters, ill health, the poor state of the roads, and other circumstances were often cited as reasons to postpone his Monticello visits." But the question naturally arises, Was there a letter in which Randolph cited reasons for not coming to visit when his twin sister was at Monticello? No there was not. Isn't it more likely that Randolph would have sent a note excusing himself from the visit, than it was that the actual visit would be formally recorded? And the report states that Randolph's only recorded Monticello visit in this time period was "on his own business." Well, of course it was! Randolph had Thomas make out his last will and testament in 1808, a short time after Eston was born by the way, and so naturally we have a formal recording of the date! Here again, the committee raises or lowers its requirements for "documented" evidence as is necessary to admit or dismiss evidence it wishes.

Moreover, it should be noted that Randolph would be more likely to have a sexual encounter with Sally than would Thomas. Randolph was known to socialize with the black slaves at Monticello when he visited there. Isaac Jefferson, in his "Memoirs of a Monticello Slave," as dictated to Charles Campbell, made the following statement:

> "Old Master's brother, Mass Randall, was a mighty simple man: used to come out among black people, play the fiddle and dance half the night; hadn't much more sense than Isaac." (JB p 22)

And we know that social occasions can easily be the occasion for two people to get together, and that they are more likely to lead in that direction than a chance contact. And since Randolph was a widower at the time, it is easy to understand how he could become involved with one of the beautiful house servants who had already had several illegitimate children. In addition, Randolph was age 51 when Eston was conceived, while Thomas Jefferson was a more elderly 64. Randolph remarried a year after Eston was born, and fathered an additional son in that marriage, so he was evidently still sexually active throughout this time period. The report in Appendix J dismisses this evidence of Randolph's socializing, saying Isaac left Monticello in 1797, and the story "most likely refers to the 1780s"—a time when Randolph had a wife—rather than later, after the evidence indicates Randolph was widowered, though the report offers no evidence for its assumption.

Then there follows a most revealing statement. The report says, "nor has anyone, until 1998, ever before publicly suggested them [i.e., Randolph and sons] as possible fathers." One could hardly expect to see such a naive declaration of incompetent thinking from a supposedly professional source. Notice that the committee requires for this evidence a *public* announcement. That means the statement by Rebecca Lee McMurry cannot be considered as evidence. (McMurry testified in a notarized statement that her family's oral tradition affirms Randolph Jefferson as the father of Sally's children.) Their approach means the committee disqualifies any evidence that was not generally known at an earlier time. It is as if, when one is trying to solve a problem or get to the bottom of an enigma, one cannot look for a solution except amongst the theories and suppositions that have already been proposed and publicly aired 200 years ago! It would be just as intelligent to suggest that DNA evidence should not be offered because it was unknown in the 19th century! This is arbitrary nonsense! But it is a good example of the incompetent, unprofessional approach which the committee took in this research study.

The report lists in Appendix J the names of several Jeffersons beside Randolph who were present at Monticello during the time when Sally conceived Eston and some of her other children. Thomas Jefferson Jr., Randolph's son, was born in 1783, and was a "resident at Monticello for extended periods of schooling in 1799, 1800 and possibly 1801." That means he apparently was present when Sally's unnamed child (who may have been named Thenia) was conceived in March 1799, and when Harriet II was conceived in August or September 1800.

Robert Lewis Jefferson, another son of Randolph, was born in 1787 and was known to have carried a letter to Monticello intended for Thomas Jefferson "in July or August 1807," according to the report. Jefferson arrived back at Monticello on August 4. The letter was dated July 9, but Jefferson did not receive it until August 8. And since Sally conceived Eston in this same time period, Robert Lewis Jefferson apparently was present at Monticello during conception time.

We must bear in mind that both of these young men had the Jefferson Y chromosome and probably the physical characteristics. Thomas Jr. would have been 17 when Harriet II was conceived, and Robert would have been 20 when Eston was conceived. It is odd that the committee considered Thomas Jr. and Robert "unlikely fathers because of their youth and very intermittent presence," at a time when Sally was 26 or 27, i.e., ten years older than the former, and 34, or fourteen years older than the latter, yet they did not consider Sally too young for Thomas Jefferson, who was thirty years older than she, and a genuinely old man of 64 when Eston was conceived. When we consider that Thomas Jr. and Robert were of an age that placed them at the height of their sexuality, one or both of them would seem to be much more likely a father for Sally's children than Thomas Jefferson himself. And as for the "intermittent presence" of Randolph's sons, we can be sure that even occasional visits would be enough to establish a sexual relationship between two persons, and even a one-night stand would be sufficient to result in the conception of a child. The committee, however, seems fixed on the idea that there had to be an ongoing relationship, and for that reason refused to consider the perfectly reasonable possibility that Sally's children were the result of various encounters.

George Jefferson, Jr., a descendant of Field Jefferson, served as Thomas Jefferson's commission agent in Richmond. It is reasonable to assume that he would have made at least occasional visits to Monticello to consult with Thomas Jefferson on business. Moreover, these visits would have occurred during the time period when Sally was bearing her children, "although no reference to such visits has yet been found," according to the Research Report. Is it possible to imagine that George Jefferson, Jr., served as Thomas Jefferson's business agent in Richmond, roughly 70 miles away, and *never* came to Monticello to discuss business? But if we demand formal records for a visit by family members, that is the conclusion that must be drawn.

John Garland Jefferson studied under the direction of Thomas Jefferson in the early 1790s, and did not marry until 1800. His visits to Monticello would surely have coincided with Thomas Jefferson's presence there.

One other son of Randolph Jefferson—Isham Jefferson—was born in 1781, and was reported to have been "reared" by Thomas Jefferson. He would have been age 26 when Eston, the last of Sally's children, was conceived. Little more than that is known about his presence at Monticello. The Research Report states that "no reference to him [Isham Randolph Jefferson], however, has yet been found in Thomas Jefferson's papers." In fact, there is indeed a reference to Isham coming to Monticello which these researchers missed. It is in Jefferson's deposition of 1815, given with reference to the probate of the last will and testament of Randolph (senior). Jefferson states in the deposition that Isham Randolph Jefferson came to speak to him about some financial problems related to his father and his father's second wife. Needless to say, that visit was not recorded in any formal register of family visits, which seems to be what the committee requires to accept the possibility that a visit occurred.

The point of all this is, however, that there were a number of Jeffersons who were around Monticello much of the time, and the fact that no notice of their presence appears in a formal register means nothing. Visits from nearby relatives were not likely to be noted unless there was something special going on in connection with the visit, especially if those relatives were frequent visitors. We would never have known that Isham was at Monticello in 1815 except for the fact that his visit had a material relationship to the subject of Jefferson's deposition.

Thus, we see from all the above that Monticello was virtually crawling with Jeffersons who could have been the father of one or more of Sally's children, all of whom had the telltale Y chromosome. And only a rigid, naive perspective would assume that the owner of a plantation was the only person who could father children by black slaves. The plantation functioned like a social microcosm, not a rigidly controlled personal harem, and the young white men who lived or visited there were just as likely as the owner to have a sexual relationship with the unmarried slave women, if not more so. In the case of an owner who was up in age, such as Thomas Jefferson, the younger men were undoubtedly more likely to have such illicit affairs. In fact, a visiting white workman at Monticello was thought to have fathered a child by one of Sally's sisters, indicating casual sexual relationships developed easily on the plantation.

One interesting point made by one of the DNA consultants, and duly ignored by the Foundation, was a concern that the match between the Eston Hemings descendant and the Field Jefferson descendants was predicated on the results gathered from a single descendant of Eston. According to one consultant, there is a danger that there could have been a "bookkeeping" error—a mix-up of test tubes, a mistake in labeling—that might have resulted in the single match that was reported. Since an error of this magnitude would have astounding results on the conclusions drawn from the testing, one would think that a dedicated researcher would be interested in following the advice given and have the single Eston descendant retested. Or perhaps extraordinary efforts could be made to locate another Eston Hemings male-line descendant so that this enormously important finding might not rest on the blood from a single living person. The testing of a descendant of Madison Hemings would also lend some collateral support to the original findings. But no. The researchers have gotten the results they were looking for, and they would rather waste time testing yet another Tom Woodson descendant (thus making a total of six!) rather than do something to put their investigation on more solid scientific grounds. Dr. Foster reported that there were other Eston descendants, but he did not bother to test them, since the first one yielded the results he was looking for. It apparently never occurred to him that the Jefferson Y chromosome could have been introduced illegitimately somewhere along the line of descent, and that it would be good scientific practice to test other descendants in order to make the evidence more reliable.

2. **No DNA match with descendants of Eston and Carr.** The report states that Jefferson's grandchildren claim that the Carrs were the fathers of Sally's and one of her sister's children, and "The DNA study contradicts these statements in the case of Sally Hemings' last child, Eston." Which, of course, is true. But that does not necessarily mean that the Carr brothers were not father to some of the other children of Sally. Certainly, unmarried women who have multiple children may have them by multiple fathers. And in fact, Sally's own mother and two of her sisters each had multiple children by multiple fathers. So this would be nothing unusual in the Hemings family. But the report then states, in effect, that because Sally's patterns of conception match Jefferson's presence at Monticello, that should be taken as evidence that *all* her children were by the same father, i.e., Thomas Jefferson. In this way, the committee uses one assumption to support another.

But this is still a dubious claim. It should be plain to anyone who gives it a second thought, that other Jeffersons were many times more likely to come to Monticello for a visit when Thomas Jefferson was there, rather than when he was away. In the January 2000 issue of *William and Mary Quarterly*, Fraser D. Neiman dismisses the possibility of some other father being at Monticello only when Jefferson is there with a footnote, rigidly adhering to the dictates of his statistical model:

> "Because the model outcomes are tabulated against Jefferson's arrival and departure dates, the probabilities that result apply to Jefferson or any other individual with identical arrival and departure dates. The chances that such a Jefferson *doppelganger* existed are, to say the least, remote."

A less pedantic approach to the problem would recognize that "any other individual" could be the father of Sally's children without necessarily having "identical arrival and departure dates" with Thomas Jefferson. Such an individual only need be there when Sally conceived. Thus we see that the author naively reveals his bias and relates the alternative possibility, not to Sally's conception dates, but to Thomas Jefferson's presence! Moreover, the statistical model does not even take into consideration the fact that Thomas Jefferson was present at Monticello on as many occasions when Sally could have conceived but did *not,* as he was when she did conceive. It begins to appear obvious that the model was set up to produce the desired results, and was not realistically designed to take into consideration other possible explanations. It was designed to indict Jefferson, and it should come as no surprise that the conclusion confirmed such a high probability as was "discovered" by such a ruse.

Thus in saying all the children were fathered by Thomas Jefferson, the report seeks to support one dubious supposition with another equally dubious. And by a similar sleight-of-hand, it tries to say that since all Sally's children had one father, and since there is no evidence of anyone other than Thomas Jefferson being at Monticello on such a constant basis, therefore "evidence of the sort of sustained presence necessary to have resulted in the creation of a family of six children is entirely lacking." That could be called begging three questions at the same time. And incidentally, we note how the committee uses the assumption of a "sustained presence" to eliminate the possibility of multiple fathers, but forgets about that kind of assumption when evaluating Edmund Bacon's eyewitness evidence.

3. No DNA match with descendants of Tom Woodson and Field Jefferson. This was perhaps the most salient result to emerge from the DNA tests. Had there been a match, then it would have been as conclusive a proof as possible that Thomas Jefferson was the father of a child of Sally, since he was the *only* Jefferson in Paris when Sally's first child was conceived. *But there was no match!* This forced proponents of an affair to backtrack and say that, well... maybe Tom Woodson was never at Monticello, even though he was specifically named by James Callender in 1802! It is important to remember that just because someone lies or makes an error, that does not mean that every word they wrote is necessarily a lie or an error. And it must also be remembered that paternity is frequently an indiscernible fact, whereas the existence or non-existence of a person is something that *is* definitely knowable. Paternity is a perfect subject for gossip, because who can prove it one way or another? But saying there is a 12-year-old boy living at the plantation is not that kind of a statement.

Madison Hemings, whose Memoirs never mentions James Callender or his accusations, claims that Sally's first child died, even though there is no record of the death. Of course, all of this happened years before Madison was even born, at a time when he could not possibly know the facts he was relating of his own knowledge. Therefore, his evidence was little more than gossip. And what about the strong oral tradition of the Woodson family? Their oral tradition should be given more credence than anyone else's, because much of it presumably was based on Tom Woodson's own knowledge and observation, not on what he had been told by someone else.

Nevertheless, the report states that "No documents have yet been found to support the belief that Woodson was Sally Hemings' first child, born soon after her return from France." And here we see how the committee arbitrarily selects or rejects evidence based on how well it fits their preconceived theory. Never mind that Callender specifically identified Tom. Never mind that the Woodson oral tradition is more firmly established and from a more reliable source (Tom Woodson) who supposedly was there and knew firsthand about most of what he spoke, as compared to Madison's account, the essentials of which occurred many years before he was even born. This is all considered as nothing worthy of consideration by the committee. But we are compelled to ask, in the wake of the above supportive evidences, "Were there any documents found to support the committee's belief that Tom Woodson was some other woman's child?" No, there were not.

4. **Sally's birth patterns and Jefferson's presence.** The report states that "the observed correlation between Jefferson's presence at Monticello and the conception windows for Hemings's known children is far more likely if Jefferson or someone with an identical pattern of presence at and absence from Monticello was the father." But as we saw above, any other possible father is much more likely to be at Monticello when Jefferson was there, rather than when he was away. And that person need not be present and absent exactly when Jefferson was present and absent. He only need be present when Sally conceived!

One of the great mysteries related to the reputed birth patterns is, If Thomas Jefferson had an affair with Sally that started in France, and if that union produced a child that was born after their return to Monticello, the birth occurring sometime in early 1790, then why were there no more children born for almost six years? The remaining group of Sally's children were all closer together. Moreover, this being supposedly the start of an affair, one would not expect to find such a great amount of delay between births at the very beginning. Of course, if we accept as fact that Thomas Jefferson was *not* the father of Sally's first child, then this makes much more sense: the child's father was some other person in France, and he did not accompany Sally on her return to America, so there were no more births immediately afterward. Moreover, that possibility finds support in the DNA evidence, and in the Woodson family history, since the Woodsons claim to be descended from that child, and the DNA evidence proves conclusively that Jefferson was not the father.

The committee solved the problem of Sally's long hiatus at the beginning of the affair by declaring Sally's first child, reportedly conceived in France and born in this country in 1790, and everything connected therewith to be a mystery. They begin calculating Sally's pregnancies with the first child conceived *in this country,* beginning in December of 1794.

Whereas such amateurish manipulation of the evidence may avoid certain problems in dealing with a difficult, confusing, and contradictory situation, we think that handling a fundamental aspect of the overall problem in that manner disqualifies the committee from proposing any kind of solution or position on the issues. We feel that the non-match between Jefferson descendants and Tom Woodson descendants demonstrates that Thomas Jefferson was *not* the father of at least one child that was said to be Sally's, and for the committee to simply avoid grappling with the issue demonstrates their incompetence and their inability to deal with any evidence except that which can be made to fit their biases and their preselected theory. The paternity of Tom Woodson is a potentially important issue because if he was Sally's first child, then the DNA evidence leads to the conclusion that there was no 38-year-long affair that began in France, Madison's "Memoirs" were a pack of lies, and Sally had her children by multiple fathers.

Common sense dictates that Monticello would be flooded by persons whose presence was almost surely to coincide roughly with Jefferson's. Moreover, there were as many times when Jefferson was present and Sally could have gotten pregnant, but did not, as there were when he was present and she did. And the calculation of those times omits the first year after childbirth, when lactating women are usually not fertile. Putting all those factors together, we begin to see that Sally's conceptions had a certain amount of randomness to them, within the confines of the times that she would be likely to conceive at all, that is, when Jefferson and his entourage were there.

An interesting pattern occurred the year Eston was conceived. Thomas Jefferson had access to Sally at two different times in the year in which she conceived Eston: he was at Monticello between April 10 and May 16, and between August 4 and October 3. But Sally did not conceive Eston during the first time period, when there is no definite evidence that any Jefferson other than Thomas had access. Rather, Sally conceived in August of 1807, when there is very good evidence that his brother Randolph was there.

More precisely, if we take 267 days as the normal time of gestation (from impregnation to birth) with a normal range from 250 to 285 days, then the normal date of impregnation for a birth occurring on May 21, 1808, would have been August 28, 1807, with a normal range between August 11 and September 15. Randolph had been invited to come to Monticello to visit with his twin sister on August 12, therefore his likely time of visiting would have been exactly within the range of time in which Sally would normally have conceived. This combination of evidence would tend to suggest that Thomas Jefferson was *not* the father of Eston, since Eston was *not* conceived at a time when evidence suggests only Thomas was at Monticello. Rather Eston was conceived only after Randolph was added to the list of those present.

The report states in Appendix F that "There is no record that Sally Hemings was anywhere but at Monticello from 1790 to 1826." This is a curious way of stating it, because we suspect that documentary evidence for her presence *or* absence was incidental at best, as it would have been for most of Randolph and his sons' comings and goings. Yet the committee seems willing to assume Sally's presence without documentary evidence that she was there, and unwilling to accept Randolph's presence, even when incidentally inferred. But this is just another example of how the committee adjusted the standard of evidence in order to support their predetermined theory.

In addition, we know, as stated in Appendix F of the report, that shortly before Martha Jefferson Randolph's death, she "reminded them [her sons] that the Hemings who most resembled Jefferson could not have been his child, since he and Sally Hemings were 'far distant from each other' for fifteen months before the birth." That has always been assumed to be an error, since we know where Thomas Jefferson was every day of his adult life, and he was at Monticello when Sally conceived all of her children. But perhaps the error was in the assumption that relates this to Thomas Jefferson's presence. The research report assumes that Sally was at Monticello constantly from 1790 to 1826. But Martha's statement suggests that she may have had information indicating that Sally was *not* present at Monticello when one of the sons was conceived, and therefore Thomas Jefferson's presence at Monticello would *not* have meant that he could father Sally's child. This is a possibility that apparently has not been explored, since proponents of an affair assume that Martha was either mistaken or lying.

5. Several neighbors believed that Jefferson fathered Sally's children. The word for this, of course, is GOSSIP. None of these people had any way of knowing from their own knowledge that Thomas Jefferson and Sally Hemings had a sexual relationship. And if they did know, that explanation was never a part of their story. At best, they passed on a story that they had gotten from someone else, or that was based on their own or others' imagination and supposition. There are many fathers who are not sure that their legal children are actually their natural children. Persons outside the bedroom can only be even less sure of paternity. So, without some kind of accompanying explanation for why an outside person happens to "know" that some man is the father of some woman's child, the accusation cannot be taken as anything other than their own suppositions or the repeating of hearsay and gossip.

All of this is the weakest kind of evidence, and should not be considered evidence at all by a serious investigative committee. It was the product of overactive imaginations, just as it has continued to be in our time with the books by Fawn Brodie and Annette Gordon-Reed. Both of these authors filled their pages with scores of "might-have-been" suppositions and assumptions. And that, no doubt, is what was done 200 years ago. Indeed, a likely source of all this gossip was inadvertently explained in the report, under the section on Family Resemblances: "It was evidently their very light skin and pronounced resemblance to Jefferson that led to local talk of Jefferson's paternity." And there in a nutshell is the whole story. This was the source of the gossip and of Callender's accusations, and this was what led to the present-day controversy. When Callender wrote, "There is not an individual in the neighbourhood of Charlottesville who does not believe the story, and not a few who know it," he was talking about gossip and hearsay, not evidence. Whatever the individuals in the neighborhood believed about Sally being a concubine of Thomas Jefferson, they could not possibly know it of their own knowledge. It was conjecture created by wagging tongues, based on a prurient imagination.

In appearance, some of Sally's children were nearly white, and one was thought to resemble Jefferson. That alone was enough to set the tongues of gossips wagging. The next step was to assume that they must be his children. And once the gossip gained the authority of appearing in print and being voiced abroad, it was a simple matter for it to be incorporated into "Family Oral Tradition" and the diary of an acquaintance. Since slaves of the time had a great tendency to attach themselves to their masters by adopting their names, it was a simple thing for an unmarried mother to tell her children that the master of the plantation was their father. If this was already talked about and published in the newspapers, this made the claim almost unavoidable. Under such circumstances, if a mother were to tell her children that the master was *not* their father, the children would probably reply, "But everybody says he is!"

So it is easy to see how this sort of gossip could get started. All of that, plus the example of the Woodson family tradition and their belief that Jefferson was the father of Tom Woodson—something conclusively proved to be false by the DNA tests—should make us very wary of any kind of neighborly gossip and family oral tradition.

John Cocke claimed that Jefferson fathered mulatto children, but he provided no explanation for *why* he thought this. Unlike Edmund Bacon, who had a reason to back up his statement, Cocke could only be repeating gossip that he picked up from neighbors. There is absolutely nothing intrinsic to his "evidence" to make it worthy of any consideration at all. And Israel Jefferson could hardly have had more to substantiate his backup of what Madison had said. Israel was not a house servant, and most of whatever knowledge he had of what was going on there was no doubt gained from others. He was a friend of Madison Hemings, and was probably prompted by the interviewer when giving his statement. Israel was about ten years old at the time Eston was conceived, so we can well understand what he could have known of his own knowledge about an affair. Most ten year old children do not really know where babies come from, so we could imagine with what sophistication such a child would discern that there was an affair going on between two people who were trying to conceal it. In addition, it would be inconceivable that this friend would contradict the statement that Madison had previously made. This stuff is as close to non-evidence as we can get.

6. **Madison claimed that Thomas Jefferson was the father of all Sally's children.** The statement made by Madison Hemings in 1873, as already noted, contained information that he could not have known firsthand, and that he had to have gotten from some other person. It contains nothing to indicate how he knew the things he was relating, and even the Research Report in Appendix F includes the statement that Madison "did not specifically mention when or how he learned the identity of his father." Apparently, Thomas Jefferson acted towards him in no way that would indicate that he was Madison's father. Moreover, his statement was intended for a publication with political motivations that were anti-Jefferson. The statement itself was not Madison's original writing, neither did it attempt to reproduce his exact words (as was done with the story by Isaac in Bear's *Jefferson at Monticello*). Rather, it was rewritten by the editor, and for that reason the exact words cannot be taken as authentic. We have no idea the extent to which the editor smoothed-out inconsistencies in the original story.

This story by Madison is treated as something unique, as an unusual piece of evidence. But the truth is, there are other descendants of Monticello slaves who also claimed that Thomas Jefferson was their forefather. And recently, another black family has claimed to be descended from George Washington, even though the best evidence indicates he was sterile, since his wife had children by a previous marriage, although George and Martha were not able to have any. These attempts to claim a great man of previous times as one's ancestor are common, and should be scrutinized carefully before being accepted as evidence. At best, they can only be used to lead one to substantial evidence. And if that substantial evidence is not present, then this kind of hearsay should be disregarded.

But always, as previously noted, it must be remembered that it is not possible for third parties to make an absolutely certain assumption about who is the father of an unmarried woman's child, unless the mother and father are living together openly, or the father acknowledges the child, or some certain evidence supports the claim. As a result, statements like Madison's concerning the parentage of himself and his siblings—facts that he could not possibly know of his own knowledge—should be viewed at most as evidence of what was believed by the speaker, and not as real evidence establishing the facts spoken.

The Research Report repeats the same fallacious point seen before: "Even the statements of those who accounted for the paternity of Sally Hemings' children differently (Thomas Jefferson Randolph, Ellen Randolph Coolidge, and Edmund Bacon) never implied that Hemings' children had different fathers." *So what?* The investigators do not seem able to comprehend that, when seeking the solution to a problem, the fact that people in the past did not anticipate a given solution is irrelevant and should not hinder people living today from reaching a reasonable conclusion just because it was not thought of before. We must also bear in mind that investigators today often have available to them evidence that was not available to individuals living at the time events occurred. For example, how many of the people living at that time knew that Randolph had been invited to be at Monticello in the time period when Eston was conceived? Later investigators are often able to discover evidence and make connections that would never have occurred to persons back then.

But this same point about something not having been mentioned previously is made at several different places in the report. In the "Assessment of Possible Paternity of Other Jeffersons" it is said that "In almost two hundred years since the issue first became public, no other Jefferson has ever been referred to as the father." Again, what difference does that make? As we have pointed out, paternity is the kind of thing that persons not a part of the relationship can only guess at. And sometimes, even the parties to the relationship are not sure. Is the Foundation incapable of entertaining a new idea, a new way of looking at things? The committee's attitude on this issue is a most unscientific one, and borders on being silly. What it clearly reveals is the workings of a biased mind set on throwing up any excuse in a dogged effort to support its theory. This uninformed assumption that a solution must have been proposed in the past in order to be acceptable today cannot be given credence in a search for truth.

The fact that the Hemings family seemed to be close-knit, and named their children after one another is another example of an irrelevancy. No doubt Sally, as the matriarch of the family, is responsible for their close-ness, and paternal consanguinity has nothing whatsoever to do with it. Closeness is a function of the family culture, not of blood. It is not uncommon for social workers to see a mother with five children having five different fathers, and being just as close and supportive of one anoth-er as a similar family with one father. And if Sally's children did not *know* that they had different fathers, that would produce the same result. In any case, such flimsy, ambiguous evidence is hardly worth serious atten-tion when the endeavor is to find evidence that supports paternity. That kind of evidence can only leave the impression that the committee has a theory, and are marshaling every kind of inconsequential evidence they can find to support it.

The report then adds, "there is no documentary evidence that Thomas C. Woodson was Sally Hemings' son." We wonder at the arbitrary stan-dard the committee adopts for evidence. Apparently, if someone had jotted down in a diary, "Tom Woodson is Sally's son," that would be con-sidered evidence by the committee. But if James Callender publishes in a public newspaper the same information and no one refutes it, even though they might negate other things that Callender wrote, then that is *not* considered "documentary evidence." There are few things in this report that make less sense.

7. **Unique access to freedom.** Thomas Jefferson Randolph declared that Sally Hemings and her children were *not* treated differently from others. Nevertheless, they were house servants, and they had some degree of status above other servants on the plantation. Sally's children were "put to some mechanical trade at the age of fourteen," according to Madison Hemings. The fact that certain considerations were expressed by giving two of Sally's children their freedom and allowing them to "run away," and that the remaining two were given their freedom in Jefferson's will (together with three other Hemings-related servants who were not Sally's children) should not be viewed as anything extraordinary. It should be noted that Sally herself was not given her freedom in Jefferson's will, so these manumissions show no evidence of special favoritism to Sally. It is easy to conceive of all of this being done without any special promise to Sally, or any extraordinary attempt to reward her remaining two sons.

Many reasons exist for Jefferson to do this, and those reasons do not suggest that Jefferson was their father.

In addition to being a house servant, Sally was supposedly the half-sister of Jefferson's wife, which would make Sally Jefferson's sister-in-law, and her children his niece and nephews! There is no evidence, other than the statements by Madison Hemings and Isaac Jefferson, for believing that John Wayles was the father of Sally Hemings, and some historians do not believe this was true. But if it is true, we know that the Carr brothers, who lived for some time at Monticello, were Jefferson's nephews, and he was careful to look after them. If Sally's children were the children of his wife's half-sister, should we be surprised that Jefferson made special allowances for these closely-related servants? Indeed, we might expect them to be virtual family members, and to receive special consideration in training and the assignment of tasks.

The fact that, as the report states, "Jefferson gave freedom to no other nuclear slave family" is meaningless, because it is only to be expected with this particular family. Jefferson had enormous debts, and freeing all his slaves was beyond his power, since all his property was mortgaged, and slaves were considered property in those days. But it is interesting to note that in freeing these Hemings servants, he did so roughly in accordance with a plan he outlined in his "Notes on Virginia" when Sally was less than ten years old. What Jefferson was doing with the Hemingses, therefore, was a modified form of the emancipation he had proposed for *all* slaves before Sally even went to France, years before any of her children were even born. It was the *children* of slaves who were to be freed, and that was to be done after they received a level of training that enabled them to continue as free persons.

Moreover, Sally's children were not the only servants freed. Burwell Colbert, Joe Fosset, and John Hemings were also freed in Jefferson's will. But that doesn't make Jefferson their father. All were freed for several discernible reasons, but as Elizabeth Langhorne points out, there was one thing that all those who were freed had in common: "By no means did these five represent the whole Hemings connection; they were those whom Jefferson believed could go it alone in the white world." (EL p. 256) That was important to Jefferson, who no doubt had second thoughts about freeing slaves when he saw what happened to James Hemings, Sally's brother who had gone with Jefferson to France. James was freed in 1796, and even though he had training for a trade, he nevertheless had trouble finding and keeping a job, ended up an alcoholic, and committed suicide five years after being freed, in 1801.

8. Madison Hemings family history. The committee constantly put enormous emphasis on oral family tradition. The fact that Madison's family story was printed in the *Pike County (Ohio) Republican* in 1873 no doubt tended to stabilize this story as a piece of family tradition to be passed down from generation to generation. But why the report should list this fact as a separate, and presumably important, "uncontested historical fact" apart from Madison's statement itself seems curious. Perhaps this results from the Foundation's emphasis on oral family tradition with their "Getting Word" project. This Madison Hemings family history, the report is careful to point out, was passed down "despite a climate of hostility and denial," as though this level of tribulation somehow adds veracity to the story.

In professional genealogical circles, oral family tradition is given no credence at all, except perhaps to direct an investigator to substantial documented sources that are considered the only reliable genealogical materials. The present experience with the Woodson family tradition well illustrates how unreliable such stories can be. The Woodsons are adamant that they are descended from Thomas Jefferson. But if the Woodsons are wrong about being descended from Thomas Jefferson in spite of their extremely strong tradition and beliefs, is it not equally possible that the other Hemings descendants are also mistaken? On questions concerning the paternity of an unmarried woman's children, oral family tradition is probably the most unreliable evidence that exists.

9. Family resemblances. Here again is another weak piece of evidence. The fact that Eston almost certainly had Jefferson blood in his veins, as indicated by the DNA tests, would cause one to expect that he might have a resemblance to the Jeffersons, including Thomas. The 12-year-old boy Tom (Hemings) Woodson was also said to resemble the President, and we now know from the DNA tests that there was no connection to the Jefferson family at all. These "facts," in and of themselves are ambiguous, have no great significance, and do not necessarily establish a paternal con-nection to Thomas Jefferson. If Thomas were the *only* Jefferson that could have been the father, and the question was whether it was he or some other non-Jefferson-looking male, *then* perhaps this "look-alike" evidence might have some slight significance. But when there was a whole handful of Jeffersons that cannot be eliminated as the possible father, look-alike evidence is meaningless. Any one of them could have been the father and have produced the same result. And when there is some evidence that another Jefferson indeed was at Monticello at the time of conception, then this look-alike evidence turns out to be worthless.

The report notes that "Thomas Jefferson Randolph told Henry S. Ran-dall in the 1850s of the close resemblance of Sally Hemings' children to Thomas Jefferson." In fact, he told Randall that Sally "had children which resembled Mr. Jefferson so closely that it was plain that they had his blood in their veins." So what are we to make of this? Later on in the very same interview, T. J. Randolph told Randall "that there was not the shadow of suspicion that Mr. Jefferson in this or any other instance ever had commerce with his female slaves." This could only mean that what he meant in the first statement was, it was plain *to those who spread the rumor* that Sally's children had Jefferson's blood in their veins, or perhaps he thought the children had *Jefferson* blood in their veins, but not that of Thomas Jefferson himself. He went on to explain in that interview that he actually lived at Monticello, and he saw nothing that suggested to him that there was any familiarity between Mr. Jefferson and Sally Hemings. And, as we now know, there is good evidence that Randolph Jefferson could have been the father of at least one of Sally's children, therefore what we now know confirms *both* that at least one of her children had Jef-ferson blood, and that this blood was likely not from Thomas Jefferson.

Summary. As we can see from the above nine major pieces of "uncon-tested scientific or historical facts," there is *nothing* to directly link Thomas Jefferson as father of Sally's children. None of this is "over-whelming," and all of it can be explained easily and simply. The "evidence" that identifies Thomas Jefferson as the father is all gossip, imaginative supposition, and oral tradition, and all of those are examples of weak evidence indeed. The very strongest possible kinds of evidence—

eyewitness testimony, and the perpetrator's confessions—are both on the side of Jefferson's innocence. Therefore, weighing the two sides, and judging according to the quality of the evidence, one feels compelled to conclude that the best evidence says that Jefferson was *not* involved in an affair with Sally Hemings.

The report states that "Many aspects of this likely relationship between Sally Hemings and Thomas Jefferson are, and may remain, unclear, such as the nature of the relationship, the existence and longevity of Sally Hemings' first child, and the identity of Thomas C. Woodson." The fact is, the whole hypothesis that there was a relationship is built on inference. There is no solid evidence except that opposed to the existence of a relationship. Therefore, it is to be expected that there would be any number of loose ends and contradictions that can never be resolved, mainly because the whole story is all based on false assumptions. That the committee would issue a report saying the evidence was "overwhelming" in favor of a relationship when fundamental aspects, such as the issues surrounding Tom Woodson as Sally's first child, are unresolved only attests to the committee's wish to promote their findings regardless of the evidence. On that issue alone, a reasonable person would conclude that no position should be taken unless those questions were settled.

Absurdities and Contradictions

It became necessary for the Research Committee to gloss over all the many absurdities and contradictions engendered by the theory they adopted, which assumed that indeed there was an affair between Thomas Jefferson and Sally Hemings. Unlike real scientific solutions, their "solution" to this controversial question does not provide a *key* to understanding. It does not make all or most of the many elements of this story fall into place and make sense. Rather, just the opposite occurs: it is a forced and contorted explanation, disregarding key pieces of evidence for insubstantial reasons, varying standards of evidence to accommodate their own theory, making certain assumptions for evidence favoring their theory and reversing those assumptions for evidence not favoring their theory. They fail to view with common sense the likelihood of persons actually knowing the rumors and gossip they were repeating, and themselves repeat the unscientific fallacies and misconceptions of biased proponents of an affair. True explanations clarify a situation; they don't make it more confusing, nor do they rely on a belief that a large number of reputable people were liars in order to give substance to gossip. Here are some of the absurd and contradictory results of this disgraceful example of scholarship:

—Thomas Jefferson himself, one of the great Founding Fathers of this great nation, is made out to be a liar, a hypocrite, a child molester (if Sally had a son in 1790), a fornicator, a miscegenist, and a de facto law breaker over a period of 38 years.

— Martha Jefferson Randolph is made out to be a liar on her death bed.

— James Callender is acknowledged to be a liar, but then is also viewed as telling the truth (which was based solely on gossip).

— Oral tradition is accepted as equal or superior to personal testimony, even if the source of the tradition is unknown and cannot be verified.

— Tom Woodson, around whom the accusations started, is made never to have lived at Monticello.

— Thomas Jefferson is made to continue with this "affair" even after being exposed in the public press, even while holding the highest public office in the land, even while seeking a second term.

— Sally Hemings is assumed to be "monogamous" with respect to Thomas Jefferson, but is not "monogamous" when considering Edmund Bacon's eyewitness evidence.

— The Carr brothers confession is not considered valid because of the fact that Eston had a Jefferson as his father, Sally is assumed to have been monogamous, and therefore that eliminates the Carr brothers.

— The Carr brothers confession is also not considered valid because they made confessions on two different occasions, and they laughed at one and wept at the other.

— The Foundation's Committee set itself up to determine the facts of this controversy, yet they refused to consult with notable opponents, such as Herbert Barger or Willard Sterne Randall.

— The Foundation and its committee refused to actively pursue additional scientific evidence in the form of DNA from the deceased

William Hemings that would add a greater measure of certainty to their investigations.

With a committee of this sort, composed only of staff members of the Foundation, one would expect that they should bend over backwards in an attempt to demonstrate some kind of neutrality, open-mindedness, and even-handedness. We might even forgive them for showing a bias toward Thomas Jefferson, demanding a strict adherence to "guilty until *proven* innocent," and not accepting the *probable* existence of Jefferson's paternity of Sally's children without at least some solid, conclusive evidence that there indeed was such a connection. But that this committee, consisting of members of the Thomas Jefferson Memorial Foundation, should adopt a position supporting the enemies and calumniators of Jefferson, and that they should do this on the basis of the shoddiest, most incompetent interpretations of vague and inconclusive evidence—evidence which relies almost entirely on implications and innuendos and handed down gossip—such a betrayal of the person and reputation of the great man their Foundation was established to uphold is dastardly and unforgivable.

As the complete Research Report so carefully documents, *all* of the existing evidence related to these accusations was available to the committee. But their biased theory blinded them to the significance of the material. And this only proves that all the best evidence in the world is of no help when the minds of the investigators are closed to new leads and possibilities and to the input of ideas from those who disagree with their chosen theory.

It is understandable why the Foundation, after recording the oral history of dozens of descendants of slaves associated with Monticello, might wish to validate their story. But the fact is, each of those stories started from one person. And if that one person exaggerated, or switched the identity of a forebear, that became established as "oral tradition" and was passed on to all succeeding generations. This way of switching the identity of a forebear was well illustrated in the case of Eston Hemings' descendants, who apparently did it to make a break with their black heritage. Naturally, the Foundation feels a great sympathy with the persons who cooperated in their "Getting Word" project, and would find it repugnant to turn their back on these people and seem to consider such contributions worthless, even if that were true. *But that is all the more reason why the foundation should not have conducted this research themselves.* Or, if determined to do it in-house, they should have been especially careful to engage and listen to outside consultants and other persons with opposing views. This they evidently did not do, and this is something that would naturally tend to make their report unconsciously biased. The only "outside" consultants appear to be those who advised on the DNA results, the science of which, as one of the consultants stated, was so routine that "the DNA study does not merit a scholarly conference." Thus we have the picture of a research team, carefully engaging multiple outsiders on questions upon which everyone agrees, and just as carefully avoiding any outsiders on those aspects where there is real controversy.

While we can understand the need to validate the black experience and to help all those men and women who were once discriminated-against feel they are an authentic part of American life, we nevertheless feel that to do this by destroying the honor and reputation of one of America's greatest Founding Fathers, and discrediting the man who was the intellectual father of American democracy—a political system that has become the rallying point for freedom-loving people around the world—can do neither blacks, nor this country, nor the cause of liberty any good whatsoever. This is not the time to be denigrating our most eloquent spokesman for liberty, democracy, and freedom.

Bias is very tricky, and an honest investigator must take extraordinary steps to prevent it from sneaking in and displacing other views that might lead to a solution. As Nobel laureate and scientist Richard Feynman wrote, "The first principle is that you must not fool yourself—and you are the easiest person to fool." This describes the scientific approach, the approach of true investigators. They deliberately seek opposing views and carefully test them against their own theory, because it is through that clash of differing ideas and opinions that the truth emerges. If investigators do not do this, they run the risk of fooling themselves and ultimately undermining their own best intentions. Input from different viewpoints is needed in every endeavor. Shutting such inputs out is a prescription for disaster.

The TJMF study only illustrates the poverty of the approach taken by the historians on the Foundation staff as well as others who deliberately exclude those who disagree with them, who call them "crazy," and "flat-earthers." It should be plain to any fair minded person that if we are dealing with a controversy—and certainly the questions surrounding Thomas Jefferson and Sally Hemings are controversial!—then reasonable, intelligent people can take different sides, and one cannot hope to reach an intelligent conclusion by treating opposing views with contempt. Indeed, an intelligent investigator cherishes such opposing views, and studies them more carefully than the views of supporters, because it is through understanding the opposition that one is likely to gain new insights into one's own position.

The committee report suggests that the preponderance of the historical evidence indicates that Thomas Jefferson was the father of Sally's children, but as we have seen, this is patently false. There is not a single stitch of direct evidence linking Thomas Jefferson to the paternity of Sally's children, and every piece of so-called "evidence" can be easily explained in simple, ordinary, uncomplicated ways. No one suggests that Jefferson ever publicly or privately acknowledged Sally's children to be his—not even Madison in his statement, or Cocke in his diary, or any of the oral family traditions. From the very beginning, the whole story has been the product of gossip based on inference, supposition, and imagination. There are several pieces of good evidence indicating that Jefferson was *not* involved with Sally, and to counteract these, proponents of an affair are compelled to make all the responsible persons into liars. The only response that an open-minded, intelligent person could have to this tissue of twisted inferences is to say that it is all poppycock.

Referenced Sources

AL The Adams-Jefferson Letters: The Complete Correspondence
Between Thomas Jefferson and Abigail and John Adams.
Ed. by Cappon, Lester J.
Chapel Hill: University of North Carolina Press, 1959.

BM Bernard Mayo and James A. Bear, Jr.
"Thomas Jefferson and His Unknown Brother"
University Press of Virginia, 1981.

EL Elizabeth Langhorne
Monticello: A Family Story
Chapel Hill: Algonquin Books, 1987.

GR Annette Gordon-Reed
Thomas Jefferson and Sally Hemings: An American Controversy
Charlottesville: University Press of Virginia, c. 1997, 1999.

JB James A. Bear, Jr., ed.
Jefferson at Monticello
Charlottesville: University Press of Virginia, 1967.

Present at the Conception

David Murray, Ph.D.
Director, Statistical Assessment Service

The "most provocative finding" of The Thomas Jefferson Memorial Foundation Research Report, said *USA Today,* was a new statistical analysis that showed Jefferson's residence at Monticello when Hemings' children were conceived. This feature of the Report is the only novel information contained within it, apparently justifying the intense news coverage. In actual fact, historian Winthrop Jordan in 1968 had already demonstrated the correlation between Thomas Jefferson's Monticello presence and the conception periods of Sally Hemings, but did not dress the facts with elaborate mathematical models that appear to establish no more than correlation.

According to Fraser Neiman, an archeologist who did the mathematical analysis, "the chance is just 1% that his presence was a coincidence… How likely is it that this could have occurred by chance if Jefferson was not the father?" Neiman ran "four mathematical models to measure the probability." Neiman said to the press, "Serious doubts about his paternity of all six children cannot reasonably be sustained. This statistical analysis is more powerful…than the genetic finding." What is the finding? Between the years 1795 to 1808, Jefferson was at Monticello roughly half the time; 2,612 days at home, 2,644 days away. Six children were conceived by Hemings during the days when Jefferson was home, while none of those six were conceived while Jefferson was away. This analysis has already been subjected to the bed of Procrustes, since Thomas Woodson's birth, from an earlier period, has been dismissed from consideration. The DNA shows he was not a Jefferson descendant. But the oral history concerning him is easily the strongest of all the oral history claims. His life creates a dilemma for asserting Thomas Jefferson's paternity. Were we to acknowledge the DNA facts, they would demonstrate that slave oral history is not reliable. Worse, if Woodson were Hemings' child, conceived in Paris but not fathered by Thomas Jefferson, then Hemings demonstrably had relations with at least one other man. The Report, on the other hand, commits itself to the position that the Thomas Jefferson/Hemings' relationship was not only long term but monogamous.

Finally, truly putting a spanner in the works, a Woodson birth cannot be accommodated in the time period of Thomas Jefferson's Monticello visits in order to run the mathematical models. Since Woodson was born in 1790, and the next birth to Hemings is 1795, the Report is left having to account for a five-year sexual relationship with no results. Only two maneuvers remain open to save the appearances, the models, and the oral history. Either sustain the assertion of sex between Thomas Jefferson and Sally beginning before 1795, keeping the long term relationship (though at the expense of monogamy), but postulate numerous miscarriages, or, dismiss Woodson entirely from consideration by declaring him no child of Hemings. Remarkably, the Foundation takes both tacks in its analysis.

Woodson is excommunicated from both Thomas Jefferson and Sally Hemings, from the one by DNA results, and from the other because no documents regarding his birth to Sally can be found. This maneuver creates collateral problems in the fact that a young male said to be Thomas Woodson was attributed to live at Monticello by several observers for some years, but such testimony can be dismissed when it doesn't move in a palatable direction, especially if the press has to dig into appendixes or actual history to find it.

Be that as it may, the remaining births can indeed be fit into a mathematical model to judge the probability that all of the conceptions would happen only when Thomas Jefferson was present at Monticello. Unfortunately, there are no comparable records establishing Sally Hemings' whereabouts during the same period. The record is silent. But let us grant the coincidence at Monticello of Thomas Jefferson, Sally Hemings, and conceptions. That is, if the events of conception were distributed purely by chance, we should have expected some number of them to have occurred during periods of Thomas Jefferson's absence; the fact that none of them do implicates Thomas Jefferson. What have we learned?

A parallel discussion might make this more clear. Imagine vases were broken on six different occasions at Monticello. No vases were known to have been broken when Thomas Jefferson was away. Thomas Jefferson was home when all six vases were broken. There is evidence that some Jefferson likely broke one of the vases. There is no evidence that Thomas Jefferson or indeed any Jefferson broke any other vases. Are we willing, therefore, to subscribe to the conclusion that there is a 99% probability that Thomas Jefferson broke all six vases? Mercifully, courts of law are not likely to do so, there being no necessary connection between being present and the act of surreptitiously shattering glass.

So is it with conception in human affairs. Thomas Jefferson's presence at Monticello, if Sally Hemings was there, would in fact be a necessary condition for conception, but by no means a sufficient condition for conception. This fact can readily be established by noting that Thomas Jefferson visited Monticello a total of 22 times during the period in question, yet for 16 of those 22 visits no conceptions resulted. It may be further valuable to invoke the strict dictates of logic. The logic of Neiman's argument appears to be something like this: "If Thomas Jefferson fathered children, then Thomas Jefferson must have been present when those children were fathered. Children were fathered at Monticello. Thomas Jefferson was present at Monticello when children were fathered. Therefore, Thomas Jefferson fathered those children." But this form cannot sustain the conclusion drawn. Only if we knew that children were *never* conceived during Thomas Jefferson's presence would we have any definitive logical conclusion; to wit, "it is not the case that Thomas Jefferson fathered those children." Moreover, the logic must be applied not just to Thomas Jefferson but also to the assumed conjunction of Thomas Jefferson and Sally on the same days. Apparently, we should restate the argument in the following way: "If Sally and Thomas Jefferson are to conceive children, then Sally and Thomas Jefferson must have been together when those children were conceived. Children subsequently born to Sally were conceived when Thomas Jefferson was at Monticello. Therefore, Thomas Jefferson and Sally conceived those children."

But we notice some things that are missing. There is no evidence that Sally was present at Monticello when Thomas Jefferson was. We don't know if Sally was at Monticello when she conceived. And even if both Sally and Thomas Jefferson were at Monticello at the same time, was there someone else present at Monticello who was between Thomas Jefferson and Sally when she conceived? We simply don't know. Of course, there is no documentary evidence that Sally was away from Monticello when she conceived. That is, there is no record of her presence or absence on the days when she conceives. Likewise, there exist a fair number of documentary holes in the record regarding nearly all of the major players, since the only substantive record is Thomas Jefferson's own. But Sally is, for this argument to work, assumed to be present at all crucial junctures, even though there is no documentation of her presence. Finally, if we recall the statement of Yale University's Dr. Kidd, we realize that the proper formulation of a hypothesis to be statistically tested is a compound one: That Thomas Jefferson and Sally were both present at the times of conception, AND that no other chromosome carrier was also present.

At any account, the act of appearing at Monticello should not be viewed as itself a causal procreative act. The Report's mathematical model is likewise incapable of ruling out the prospect that Thomas Jefferson's visits to Monticello co-occurred with some other event, such as a visit by nearby brother Randolph (or any other of the crowd who traveled with the president), who comes to see his brother just when his brother is there. This is not idle speculation, since a record was found at Monticello showing an invitation to Randolph to visit Thomas Jefferson exactly coincident with one of the conception windows. But because no one has found a record of Randolph's actual arrival, the Report declines to pursue the Randolph connection.

One must remember that if there are 25 possible candidates to be the genitor of at least one of Sally Hemings' children, eight of whom are plausibly nearby, then each of them would have carried the DNA marker. However, there is no documentary evidence concerning their presence at Monticello, since Thomas Jefferson's diary only records his own movements. For others at Monticello for the relevant time frames the record is blank. It is equally possible to declare that some were present but unrecorded as it is to claim that no other Jefferson male was ever present during those time periods.

Neiman's discussion of alternatives is contained in a footnote where he says, "Because the model outcomes are tabulated against Jefferson's arrival and departure dates, the probabilities that result apply to Jefferson or any other individual with identical arrival and departure dates. The chances that such a Jefferson *doppelganger* existed are, to say the least, remote."

That point seems critical. Upon what basis did Neiman determine the "remoteness" (to say the very least, as he puts it) of that individual? Shouldn't the chances that such a one exists at least have been assayed? He needs to put some sort of value on those chances in order to attempt that which he does attempt. Even more compelling is that point that the "remoteness" seems to be a function of the assumption that either Jefferson sired all six children *or* the doppelganger is some *one* who likewise fathers all six children. Why should we assume that there is one and only one person who must tread in Jefferson's exact chronology?

That demand seems to follow from nothing more than the previously formed assumption that Sally was not promiscuous. From a probability point of view (and especially so, given the awkwardness of Thomas Woodson's paternity), there could have been doppelganger sub1, who matches Jefferson's itinerary during only one stay, and who is responsible for only one child, and then doppelganger sub 2, who matches Jefferson's itinerary on another occasion, and fathers another Hemings child, and so forth. Maybe six doppelgangers, maybe only two or three;

who knows? Moreover, maybe it's someone already at Monticello throughout the period continuously, who therefore doesn't have to "match" Jefferson's comings and goings, but is just opportunistically "there" and takes advantage during circumstances that present themselves when Jefferson is coincidentally home. And so forth. I am not arguing that we have evidence of these scenarios. But it would seem that those likelihoods must at least be specified and allowed to function in the model as alternative hypotheses, and not just be dismissed. As it stands, the argument sticks with only the most unlikely character, the one perfect Jefferson doppelganger—who presumably also wrote a parallel Declaration of Independence—who is offered as the logical alternative.

Lack of Evidence

Clearly evidence of another Jefferson's presence would have been material helping to acquit Thomas Jefferson. But does the lack of documentation strengthen the charge against Thomas Jefferson, or simply fail to provide direction one way or the other? After all, no one doubts but what some other Jeffersons, such as Randolph, were sometimes at Monticello; their presence was spoken of in the accounts of many. Yet these undoubted visits did not leave any documentary record. (Regarding the value of the absence of evidence, one is reminded of the defendant before the judge confronted with three eye-witnesses to his bank robbing. "But your Honor," he protests, "I can give you thirty people who didn't see me rob that bank.")

Opportunity, in any case, is clearly established for Thomas Jefferson, and seems neither established nor disestablished for other Jeffersons. On the part of the Monticello Foundation scholars, the absence of exculpatory documentation was treated as material in strengthening the Thomas Jefferson charge. In fact, the "opportunity" documentation constitutes the basis of their new decision to accept likely Thomas Jefferson paternity. On balance, I would judge that while the documented presence of Thomas Jefferson during the "windows of conception" cannot increase his probability of paternity, it does serve to close one loophole of potential doubt.

It is nevertheless instructive to see how the Foundation Report handles the absence of evidence in other circumstances. We don't know where Sally Hemings was at the times of conception. Of this, the Report can only say, "There is no documentary evidence suggesting that Sally Hemings was away from Monticello when Thomas Jefferson was present." That is, we see a double standard. When there is no documentary evidence that brother Randolph was there during a conception date, the Report concludes that therefore he was not. Comparably, there is no documentary evidence that Sally was at Monticello during the dates of conception. Nevertheless, the Report lists as "Unquestioned" the statement that "Sally Hemings and Thomas Jefferson were both at Monticello at the probable conception times."

By the Report's insistence, Sally Hemings is there unless proven otherwise, while Randolph is not there unless proven that he is. The same maneuver is applied to Thomas Woodson, who is dismissed as Sally's child because there is no documentation of his birth to her, even though oral history links him to Sally quite strongly. At the risk of hammering the point too hard, it is well to remember that there is no documentary evidence of Woodson or indeed any of the offspring being Thomas Jefferson's children, which fact seems only an irrelevancy to the Report.

It begins to appear that the Thomas Jefferson/Sally Hemings affair has been constructed with a great deal of supposition supported by conjecture, certainly more than has been acknowledged by those who should know better. It reads as if they were trying to buttress a foreordained conclusion, which is more the mark of a prosecutor than a trier of fact. In fact, there appears to be a vast enterprise of begging three questions at once, in the form of the following: The oral testimony, not itself convincing but when coupled with the DNA evidence, which by itself is not determinate, but when allied with the statistical analysis of Jefferson's presence at Monticello, which is not itself sufficient to demonstrate anything, but when affirmed by the oral testimony (except when it doesn't), becomes overwhelming. That is, by chaining uncertainties together in a mutually reinforcing fashion, one ends with the indubitable. (There's always the fellow who lamented that if he only had a pot, then he could have chicken stew, if he only had a chicken.)

It is hard to escape the concern that Thomas Jefferson has been enlisted, on the losing side, in a battle of cultural symbolism, where the sexual and racial elements of the story have been allowed to predominate, turning a quest for evidence into a moral referendum on the evils of slavery. Though there is a temptation to turn the findings into a political morality play, exonerating or condemning races, genders, or a nation by proxy, to do so at the expense of the facts is corrosive. The effect is to cow critics into silence by an implicit appeal to their motives. The standing of Black Americans in our shared history no more depends upon the contingencies of DNA science than it does on Jeffersonian dalliance, while the meaning of Jeffersonian ideals can neither be enhanced nor destroyed by evidence of his personal allegiance to them or his possible hypocrisy. When we are forced to accept an "official story" by means of a process more political than scientific, driven by a well-meaning desire to mythologize, we do so at the expense of the unfettered search for truth. As for whites and African Americans, once we as a united people with a shared landscape and mutual past hook our mythologized desires to contingent scientific outcomes, we thereby put both in jeopardy.

What most perplexes is to observe the ready alacrity on the part of the academic and media culture to accept Jefferson's demolition, such that it will be abetted or even conjured when it is not found in the hard evidence. The facts themselves, while arresting, were not sufficient to propel conviction were there not a prior structure, some sort of cultural overhang, looming and waiting to collapse. It seems as if all that were really necessary was for some evidence suggestive enough that whatever slender force held back the avalanche could now be kicked away. And the indeterminate DNA evidence seems to have provided just that trifle of a suggestion.

The Case Against Thomas Jefferson: A Trial Analysis of the Evidence on Paternity

Richard E. Dixon, Attorney at Law

Thomas Jefferson, the President of the United States and owner of the Virginia plantation Monticello, was accused in the Federalist press in the early 1800s of fathering children by his slave Sally Hemings. Jefferson did not issue a public denial, and the allegations did not affect his election to a second term in 1804. It does not appear to have been an issue during the remainder of his life. The rumor was resurrected in 1873 when one of Sally Hemings' sons, Madison, claimed in a newspaper interview that he and his sister Harriet and two brothers, Beverly and Eston, were Jefferson's children. In 1998, DNA testing on the descendants of Jefferson's uncle, Field Jefferson, identified a distinct chromosome Y haplotype, which was also identified by DNA tests in a single descendant of Eston Hemings. The scientific probability is that Thomas Jefferson also had this haplotype.

The issue presented for analysis is whether the results of the DNA tests and any relevant historical evidence establish that Thomas Jefferson was the father of one or more of the children of Sally Hemings.

Historians are not bound by the legal rules of evidence, of which the most striking example in the Jefferson case is the creditability given to newspaper articles and comments in third party letters. The various historical treatments of whether Jefferson could be the father of slave children generally manipulate the facts and inferences to achieve a desired conclusion. The claim of the descendants of Sally Hemings does not rest on how many historians find Jefferson's paternity plausible, but whether potential claimants are able to establish that they are lineal descendants of Thomas Jefferson. That is a legal question and must be tested by legal rules of evidence, irrespective of the passage of time.

After the DNA tests, the Thomas Jefferson Memorial Foundation, the corporation which owns Monticello, set up a research committee, selected from its staff members, which produced a report (the "Committee Report") that there was a "strong likelihood" Thomas Jefferson fathered six children by Sally Hemings. Because of the prominence Monticello has achieved, the Committee Report was anticipated as a definitive treatment of the available evidence. Instead, it is a serious example of an assault on historical truth. Not only is the evidence manipulated, but unsupported postulates are created to fill the evidentiary gaps toward an apparently desired conclusion.

This analysis will review the information known about the relationship of Thomas Jefferson and Sally Hemings on the basis of legal principles of evidence and determine what evidence would be admissible in a legal proceeding to test paternity. It is not the purpose of this analysis to prove who was the father (or fathers) of Sally Hemings' children, but to see whether the evidence will prove the paternity of Thomas Jefferson.

There have been a number of writers who have examined the character and conduct of Jefferson and concluded that he could not have maintained a relationship with one of his slaves, secret even from the closest members of his family. His granddaughter called it a "moral impossibility." Whether the "inner Jefferson" could have maintained such a relationship is not an element in this analysis; only his actual conduct is material to the issue. The historical treatments of recent writers, including the Committee Report, ignore the lack of any evidence of Jefferson's physical access to Hemings and, with the use of circumstantial evidence and supposition, conclude that Jefferson must have fathered some or all of the children.

Perhaps the lure of historical writing is to answer the unknown 'what' and 'why' of great events, but it is not the role of historians to decide questions which affect legal rights. That is a function of legal analysis and ultimately of the court system. If the children of Sally Hemings were fathered by Thomas Jefferson under the paternity laws of Virginia, the descendants of these children are entitled to certain rights. If they are not descendants of Thomas Jefferson, they are not entitled to those rights.

Legal Principles of Proof

The issue of parentage arises in two main instances: (1) descent and distribution, i.e., whether the child shall inherit from the father, or the father from the child, in the case of a child dying and possessed of an estate, and (2) support, i.e., whether a man denies he is the father and refuses to support his child. Prior to 1952, in Virginia, there was no obligation on a father to support an illegitimate child, so dictum on the nature of proof to establish paternity addressing this issue is slight. There are cases in which the issue of proof of paternity arose because a father denied parentage of a child born during the term of marriage and presumptively legitimate. Although some treatise writers conclude that the earlier standard of proof was preponderance of the evidence, a 1988 case indicated that proof was beyond a reasonable doubt. At the present time, it is clear that the standard to establish parentage for support (*Va. Code.* §20-49.4) and for descent and distribution (*Va. Code* §64.1-5.2) both require "clear and convincing evidence."

Burden of Proof

One charging paternity has the burden of proving it. The burden of proof refers to the party that must present the evidence to meet the applicable standard of proof. Since paternity is claimed by the descendants of the illegitimate children of Sally Hemings, the burden rests on them to prove paternity. This burden would shift to Jefferson, if the evidence presented by the descendants establishes a prima facie case that Jefferson was the father of all of Sally Hemings' children, or any of them.

Standard of Proof

This is the test against which the evidence is measured. The standard in Virginia requires the evidence to establish paternity to be "clear and convincing." To understand the meaning of "clear and convincing" as a test of the evidence, a review of the standards in Virginia law is helpful. The three standards in the order of difficulty are:

By the greater weight of the evidence. This is sometimes called "by the preponderance of the evidence." It is that evidence which the trier of fact finds most convincing. Testimony of one witness who is believed by the fact finder can be the greater weight of the evidence. *Smyth Brothers-McCleary-McClellan Co. v. Beresford,* 128 Va. 137, 104 SE 371 (1920); *Matthews v. LaPrade,* 144 Va. 795, 137 SE 788 (1925).

Clear and convincing evidence. This has been defined as that measure or degree of proof which will produce in the mind of the trier of fact a firm belief and conviction to the allegation sought to be established. It is intermediate, being more than a mere preponderance, but not to the extent of such certainty as is required beyond a reasonable doubt as in criminal cases. It does not mean clear and unequivocal. *Walker Agcy Aetna Cas. Co. v. Lucan,* 215 Va. 535, 540, 211 S.E. 2nd 88 (1975) (note that the word "unequivocal" does appear frequently in other cases). The requirement of proof by clear and convincing evidence is limited to cases equitable in nature, although many of the cases confuse the standard by the use of differing language (Friend, *The Law of Evidence in Virginia,* §9.9, p. 298).

Beyond a reasonable doubt. This is the test used in a criminal proceeding meaning proof to a certainty. "It is not sufficient to create a suspicion or probability of guilt, but the evidence must establish guilt beyond a reasonable doubt. It must exclude every reasonable hypothesis except that of guilt." *Allen v. Commonwealth,* 211 Va. 805, 808, 180 S.E. 2nd 513 (1971). Before the issue of parentage was a statutory procedure, this was the standard of proof for both civil and criminal cases involving parentage.

Admissibility

This is the test that determines whether the evidence may be considered, i.e., whether it is information from a source that the law permits in a legal proceeding and is material and relevant to the issues presented, and whether, because of the nature of the evidence, greater or lesser weight should be accorded to it.

Evidence to Establish Parentage

Common Law Proof

The common law is that body of principles and rules of action which derive their original authority from usages and customs and provided a basis for the judgments and decrees of the early courts.

Illegitimate Children. It is interesting to note that the Hemings children did not have a right to establish paternity under Virginia law during their lifetime. See, *Brown v. Brown,* 183 Va. 353, 355, 32 S.E. 2nd 79 (1944). The obligation for support of illegitimate children existed in Jefferson's time, but not for the children of slave women. The purpose of the statute was to allow the county to seek reimbursement for any expense incurred to support illegitimate children. *Fall v. The Overseers of the Poor of Augusta County,* 3 Munf. (17 Va.) 495; *Acts,* 1972, §18. Actions for support for illegitimate children were enacted in 1952. During their lifetime, the Hemings children could only have inherited from their mother, *Revised Code of* 1919 c.96. Illegitimate children now have rights equivalent to children born within a marriage.

Non-Access. Prior to the statutory change that permitted illegitimate children to inherit, there were no cases to establish paternity for such children. There were instances where a father might deny paternity of a child born to the mother during a valid marriage. In a case where a child born during a marriage is claimed to be the child of another, the presumption of the law is that it was legitimate, *Cassady v. Martin,* 220 Va. 1093, 266 S.E. 2d 104 (1980). "The presumption of legitimacy is not rebutted by proof of circumstances, which only create doubt and suspicion. To repel the presumption of legitimacy in any case, the evidence must be clear and positive …throughout the investigation the presumption in favor of legitimacy is to have weight and influence, and the evidence against it ought to be strong, distinct, satisfactory and conclusive . . . non access of the husband to the wife must be proved beyond all reasonable doubt." *Scott v. Hillenberg,* 85 VA 245, 7 S.E., 377 (1888).

This principle of "non-access" to deny legitimacy is an important concept. Without access to the mother, paternity is not possible. Modern scientific tests have largely eliminated access as an issue. Where tests do not reveal the identity of the father, the issue of cohabitation between the mother and father becomes important as an element to prove paternity. *T... v. T...,* 216 Va. 867, 868, 224 S.E. 2nd 148 (1976).

Standing. The Hemings descendants could not have made a claim to be heirs of Jefferson prior to the 14th Amendment to the U.S. Constitution. As slaves, they were not permitted to be witnesses in cases involving white people:

> "Any Negro or Mulatto, bond or free, shall be a good witness in pleas of the Commonwealth for or against Negroes or Mulattos, bond or free, or in civil pleas where free Negroes or Mulattos shall alone be partners, and in no other cases whatsoever." *Revised Code of* 1819, c 111§5.

Statutory Provisions

There was no common law procedure available to the descendants of Sally Hemings to establish the paternity of Thomas Jefferson. If an action is now brought it must be instituted under the current statutory procedure. The rules of authenticity, materiality, and relevance apply to all evidence. The hearsay rule may not be avoided unless recognized exceptions apply.

Establish Parentage. *Va. Code* §20-49.1[1] provides parentage may be established by:

a. Parentage of child and woman established by proof of birth.
b. Parentage between a child and a man may be established by:
   (i) Scientifically reliable genetic tests which affirm a 98% probability of paternity.
   (ii) Written statement of father and mother under oath.

Proceeding to Determine Parentage. In the event parentage is not established under *Va. Code* §20-49.1, then proceedings may be filed under §20-49.2. Jefferson and Hemings are not available for blood tests (§20-49.3), so evidence must be presented. *Va. Code* §20-49.4 sets the standard of proof as "clear and convincing" evidence, and provides "all relevant evidence" is admissible, which may include, but not be limited to:

  a. Evidence of open cohabitation
  b. Medical or anthropological evidence
  c. Scientifically reliable genetic tests, including blood tests
  d. General course of conduct to use parent's surname by the child
  e. Claiming child on income tax returns or other documents
  f. Written acknowledgment

Descent and Distribution. *Va. Code* §64.1-5.1 provides rights to property. The purposes of determining rights in and to property pursuant to any "deed, will, trust or other instrument," require that a relationship of parent and child must be established to determine succession through or from a person. It is assumed that any claim of the Hemings descendants will fall under this section.

  a. Adopted child
  b. Child resulting from assisted conception
  c. Child born out of wedlock is a child of the mother, and of the father if;
     (i) Parents participate in a marriage ceremony before or after birth, even if attempted marriage was prohibited by law, deemed null and void or dissolved by a court, or;
     (ii) Paternity is established by clear and convincing evidence, including scientifically reliable genetic testing, or
     (iii) No claim of succession based upon the relationship between a child born out of wedlock and a parent of such child, shall be recognized unless an affidavit by such child or someone acting for such child is filed within one year of the death of such parent in the circuit court of the jurisdiction where the property affected by the claimant is located and an action seeking adjudication of parenthood is filed in an appropriate circuit court within said time. One year period shall run notwithstanding the minority of the child. This limitation does not apply where the parent in question is established by a birth record, by admission of the parent before a court or in writing under oath, or by a previously concluded proceeding to determine parentage.

Burden of Proof for Child Born out of Wedlock. *Va. Code* §64.1-5.2 provides that the burden to establish the father of a child born out of wedlock shall be clear and convincing, and evidence may include:

a. Cohabitation openly with the mother during all of the 10 months immediately prior to the time the child was born.
b. Gave physician consent to put his name on a birth record of a child.
c. Allowed as a general course of conduct common use of his name by the child.
d. Claimed the child as his child on any statement filed with a government agency.
e. Admitted before a court having jurisdiction he was the father of the child.
f. Voluntarily admitted paternity in writing under oath.
g. The result of scientifically reliable genetic tests, including DNA tests.
h. Other medical, scientific or anthropological evidence based on test performed by experts.

Special Evidentiary Rules

Hearsay. Hearsay is testimony offered by someone who does not have personal knowledge that the testimony is true. Such a witness cannot be cross-examined on hearsay because the witness only knows what he has been told. *Greenland Corp. V. Allied, etc. Co.,* 184 Va. 588, 601, 35 S.E. 2d 801 (1945). For that reason, hearsay is inadmissible unless it falls within certain exceptions.

Pedigree Rule. Testimony concerning pedigree is well recognized as an exception to the hearsay rule, provided that no other better evidence can be obtained, and that the declarant or source of the witness' information was a member of the family or related to the family, whose history the fact concerned, and was deceased or out of the state. *Gregory v. Baugh,* 4 Rand (25 Va.) 611 (1827); *Gregory v. Baugh,* 2 Leigh (29 Va.) 665; *Rawles v. Bazel,* 141 Va. 734, 755, 126 S.E. 690 (1925); *Smith v. Givens,* 223 Va. 455, 459, 290 S.E. 2d 844 (1982); *Union Central Life Ins. v. Pollard,* 94 Va. 146, 155, 26 S.E. 421 (1896).

Dead Man's Statute. Admissions and declarations of deceased person, where not supported by other proof, especially when not against proprietary interest, are regarded as of little probative value. The public policy underlying *Va. Code* §8.01-397 provides that no judgment shall be rendered against an adverse party founded on uncorroborated testimony. *Cooper v. Cooper,* 249 Va. 511, 515, 457 S.E. 2d 88 (1995).

Ancient Documents. This rule merely dispenses with the authenticity of a document. The question of relevancy and admissibility as evidence is not affected by the fact the paper offered is an "ancient document." It is no more admissible on that ground than if it were a newly executed document. There is no hearsay exception for ancient documents. *Robinson v. Peterson,* 200 Va. 186, 90, 104 S.E. 2d 788 (1958); 7B Michie's Jurisprudence. *Evidence, §11;* See also, Federal Rules of Evidence 803(16) and 901(b)(8).

Oral History Syndrome. There is no provision in Virginia evidence law for admission of "oral history." Oral history is inherently hearsay and therefore inadmissible. It compounds the inherent objection to the testimony of dead men, by offering testimony through a living witness who has received testimony passed down over several generations. Courts do not lend willing ears to what dead men have said. *Sutton v. Sutton,* 194 Va. 179, 188, 72 S.E. 2d 275 (1952). Even under the Pedigree Rule exception to hearsay, it would not relieve one presenting such event or statement as historical truth from showing the time, place, and circumstances of the initial witness' statement. Contrary to the proponents of oral histories, the passage through generations does not strengthen the validity of the event or statement, but offers greater opportunities for its distortion.

Evaluation of the Evidence

Based on the rules of evidence which would control a suit to establish paternity under Virginia Law, the evidence advanced in support of Jefferson's paternity can now be considered. This trial analysis evaluates the available information on the issue whether Thomas Jefferson fathered any children with his slave Sally Hemings. It examines the admissibility of the evidence offered from witnesses, documents and expert witnesses.

Nature of the Evidence

Witnesses. This is the testimony offered by a person in court and offered for the truth of the statement. The test of truth is cross examination, which is not possible in a case where the parties and those having personal knowledge are dead. Evidence in such cases will generally be restricted to documents, but it is instructive to examine what the participants reportedly said, or whether they remained silent on the issue. Merely because a statement is in a document does not make it evidence. The sources of statements attributed to the witnesses must still be examined for admissibility and weight.

Documentary Evidence. These are documents prepared at the time by someone having personal knowledge of the truth of the statements in the document. Documents which contain information not within the knowledge of the writer are hearsay and inadmissible. Subject to certain exceptions for records, if the document is offered for the truth of its contents, the writer of the document would normally be subject to cross examination. Where cross examination is not possible, a document is generally inadmissible. Certain documents may avoid the hearsay objection and be admitted under the Pedigree Rule.

Experts. An expert may be defined briefly as one who is qualified to draw an opinion which the trier of fact, i.e., the jury, or the judge sitting without a jury, would not be qualified to draw because of the nature of the subject discussed, e.g. DNA testing. The expert is subject to cross examination and the evidence must be material and relevant.

Witnesses

Sally Hemings. Sally was born in 1773 and she traveled to Paris at about age 14, as a companion for Jefferson's youngest daughter, Mary (Polly). She returned to Monticello with Jefferson when she was about sixteen and she may have given birth shortly after the return to a son Tom, who later took the name Tom Woodson. She was the daughter of Betty Hemings, who was the slave of John Wayles. She was left with her mother under the will of John Wayles to his daughter, Martha Jefferson. It has been noted by Jefferson biographers that John Wayles may have been Sally's father, based on an article in the *Washington Federalist* of June

134

19, 1805, which stated she was the "natural daughter of Mr. Wales (sic) who was the father… of Martha Jefferson,"[2] and the 1873 interview with Madison Hemings.[3] If correct, that would make her the half sister to Martha Wayles Skelton Jefferson, the wife of Thomas Jefferson. In addition to the disputed Tom, Sally had six children, Harriet in 1795 (d. 1797), Beverly in 1798, a daughter in 1799 (d. 1800), Harriet in 1801, Madison in 1805, and Eston in 1808. Except for Tom, all of the births are recorded, one in a letter and the rest in Jefferson's Farm Book.[4] There is some dispute, however, whether there was a 1799 birth.

Area of Testimony. Sally Hemings never uttered a public or private statement of an affair with Jefferson which produced all or some of her six children over a period of some thirteen years. She lived at Monticello over thirty-five years, which was occupied by Jefferson's daughters and grandchildren, and visited by his brother, sister, nephews, and other assorted relatives, not to mention countless visitors from the outside.[5] No documents exist which provide direct proof that Thomas Jefferson was the father of any of her children.

Admissibility and Weight. The 1873 interview of Madison Hemings does not state the source of his information, and testimony of Sally Hemings through Madison would not be admissible as clearly within the hearsay rule. If admissible, under the Pedigree Rule, it would be entitled to little weight because it is not corroborated by any other statements made by Sally Hemings or any of her children or relatives. There is no evidence she ever supported the claim of Jefferson paternity.

James Thomson Callender. Callender came from Scotland in 1792, experienced in scandal writing. He was in Philadelphia for about three years where he wrote anti-federalist articles for the Philadelphia *Gazette* and *Aurora*. He became the editor of the *Richmond Recorder* and wrote a series of articles in September–December 1802, which claimed that Jefferson was the father of several children by his slave Sally Hemings and identified one a boy, Tom, about 12 years old.[6]

Area of Testimony. A number of excerpts from Callender's articles in the *Richmond Recorder* were identified in the Committee Report of the Thomas Jefferson Memorial Foundation. These summarize the Callender allegations of a Jefferson paternity.

a. *Richmond Recorder,* article of September 1, 1802:[7]

"It is well known that the man, whom it delighteth the people to honor, keeps, and for many years past has kept, as his concubine, one of his own slaves. Her name is SALLY. The name of her eldest son is TOM."

"By this wench Sally, our President has had several children."

b. *Richmond Recorder,* article of September 22, 1802:[8]

"Sally's business makes a prodigious noise here. You may save yourself the trouble of a moment's doubt in believing the story. But what will your pious countrymen upon the Connecticut say to such African amours?"

c. *Richmond Recorder,* article of November 10, 1802:[9]

"It is said, but we do not give it as gospel, that one of her daughters is a house servant to a person in this city. This wench must have been by some other father than the President."

d. *Richmond Recorder,* article of December 8, 1802:[10]

"Other information assures us, that Mr. Jefferson's Sally and their children are real persons that the woman herself has a room to herself at Monticello. . . Her son, whom Callender calls President Tom, we also are assured, bears a strong likeness to Mr. Jefferson."

Admissibility and Weight. Disgruntled because Jefferson would not appoint him to a government position, Callender's bias greatly affected his credibility. Aside from that, his writings would not be admissible under the common hearsay rule. He makes no pretense of having first-hand information, but clearly relied on "our correspondent," "other information," "it is said," "we are assured." Callender may have picked up this rumor in an earlier newspaper article,[11] but he is the principal source of the public rumors about Jefferson and Hemings, and his writings cannot constitute any evidence for paternity of any of the Hemings children since he had no personal knowledge. The rumor reported by Callender that Jefferson was the father of the boy, Tom, has been shown not to be true through the recent DNA tests. The Tom in the Callender article is the common ancestor of the Woodson family, who claim to be descendants of Thomas Jefferson. According to family tradition, Tom was conceived in Paris and born after Hemings returned to Monticello.

Beverly Hemings. He was the oldest child who survived and the first son born to Sally Hemings in 1798. Jefferson recorded in his Farm Book that Beverly ran away in 1822. His racial mix is not known, but he is assumed to have been legally white.[12] It is likely he married a white woman and after that passed for white. His descendants have not been located.

Area of Testimony. There is no known statement that he ever claimed to be the son of Thomas Jefferson.

Admissibility and Weight. There is no evidence he ever supported the claim of Jefferson paternity.

Harriet Hemings. She was the only surviving daughter of Sally Hemings, born in 1802. She left Monticello in 1822. Jefferson recorded in his Farm Book that Harriet ran away. Jefferson's overseer, Edmund Bacon, in an account that may be barred by the hearsay rule, claimed Jefferson gave her funds to assist her in leaving.[13] She married into a white family and after that passed for white. Her descendants have not been located.

Area of Testimony. There is no known statement that she ever claimed Jefferson as her father.

Admissibility and Weight. There is no evidence that she ever supported the claim of Jefferson paternity.

Eston Hemings. The youngest child of Sally Hemings was born in 1808 and was freed by Jefferson's will in 1826. He is assumed to have been legally white, and married a free woman of color, who probably was also legally white. They lived for a time as blacks in Ohio, then moved to Wisconsin and passed into white society.

Area of Testimony. The oral tradition in the Eston Hemings family was that Eston was descended from Thomas Jefferson's uncle or a nephew. There is no evidence he ever claimed paternity of Jefferson, but his descendants have raised the claim since the DNA tests. A reference to his resemblance to Jefferson was mentioned in a newspaper article in the *Daily Scioto Gazette,* August 1, 1902.[14]

Admissibility and Weight. Eston Hemings had the Jefferson haplotype, but rumors of his resemblance to Jefferson are hearsay and inadmissible.

There is no evidence that he ever supported the claim of Jefferson paternity.

James Hemings. Brother of Sally Hemings, he accompanied Jefferson to Paris in 1783 and returned with him in 1790. He would have been witness to Sally's pregnancy which occurred in Paris and which may have resulted in the birth of the boy Tom upon their return to Monticello. He was freed by Jefferson in 1796.

Area of Testimony. James never claimed that Jefferson was the father, either of Tom or subsequent children born to Sally before James' death, i.e., a daughter who did not survive in 1795, Beverly in 1798, a possible daughter who did not survive in 1799, and Harriet in 1801.

Admissibility and Weight. There is no evidence that he ever supported the claim of Jefferson paternity.

Tom Woodson. According to the oral history of the Woodson family, he was the child born to Sally Hemings shortly after her return from Paris. DNA evidence has shown that he was not the son of Thomas Jefferson. There are no records of his birth at Monticello. It is not known why he believed he was the son of Thomas Jefferson.[15]

Area of Testimony. The DNA evidence proves that he was not the son of Thomas Jefferson.

Admissibility and Weight. It is not material to the issue of Jefferson paternity whether Tom Woodson was the son of Sally Hemings. The oral history of the Woodson family would not be admissible to contradict the DNA evidence.

Documentary Evidence

Letters of Thomas Jefferson. A series of articles authored by James T. Callender appeared in the *Richmond Recorder* in 1802 which charged that Jefferson had a slave mistress who produced five children.[16] The articles were repeated by other papers sympathetic to Federalist policies. There is no record of Jefferson ever mentioning Sally Hemings by name other than in his farm accounts. His views are well known that he resisted response to personal attacks. He did, however, issue a number of denials which would be inclusive of these allegations. The authenticity of these letters is not disputed. *Va. Code* §8.01-279.

a. Letter from Jefferson to John Tyler, June 28, 1804. Tyler was a judge of the General Court at this time and later governor of Virginia. He had been a friend of Jefferson since they were students at William & Mary.[17]

> "Amidst the direct falsehoods, the misrepresentations of
> truth, the calumnies and the insults resorted to by a faction to
> mislead the public mind, and to overwhelm those entrusted
> with its interests, our support is to be found in the approving
> voice of our conscience and country, in the testimony of our
> fellow citizens, that their confidence is not shaken by these
> artifices. When to the plaudits of the honest multitude, the
> sober approbation of the sage in his closet is added, it
> becomes a gratification of an higher order. It is the sanction of
> wisdom superadded to the voice of affection. The terms,
> therefore, in which you are so good as to express your satisfac-
> tion with the course of the present administration cannot but
> give me great pleasure."

Admissibility and Weight. Written to a close friend about two years after the Callender allegations, this is one of the first expressions by Jefferson that truth will overcome the "direct falsehoods" directed to him. This is a statement which encompasses the Callender allegations and would be admissible.

b. Letter from Jefferson to James Sullivan, May 21, 1805. Sullivan later became Governor of Massachusetts.[18]

> "If we suffer ourselves to be frightened from our post by
> mere lying, surely the enemy will use that weapon; for what
> one so cheap to those whose system of politics morality makes
> no part? The patriot, like the Christian, must learn that to
> bear revilings & persecutions is a part of his duty; and in pro-
> portion as the trial is severe, firmness under it becomes more
> requisite and praiseworthy. It requires, indeed, self command."

Admissibility and Weight. The personal attacks against Jefferson, revived in 1804, were apparently sparked by his election, prompting a number of statements from Jefferson that revealed the pain he felt from the charges. Since the 1802 charges by Callender continued to be a part of the Federalist assault on Jefferson's character this letter would encompass Callender's charges, and would be admissible.

c. Cover letter from Jefferson to Secretary of the Navy, Robert Smith, July 1, 1805.[19]

> "You will perceive that I plead guilty to one of their charges, that when young and single I offered love to a handsome lady. I acknoledge its incorrectness. it is the only one founded in truth among all their allegations against me."

Admissibility and Weight. This cover letter apparently was attached to a more detailed private letter of denial which has not survived. It is almost a direct statement to the Callender claims by the principal party to the case who denies the allegations in issue and would be admissible.

d. Letter from Jefferson to William Duane, March 22, 1806. Duane was the publisher of the Philadelphia newspaper, *Aurora.*[20]

> "Instead of listening first, then doubting, lastly believing anile tales handed round without an atom of evidence, if my friends will address themselves to me directly, as you have done, they shall be informed with frankness and thankfulness. There is not a truth on earth which I fear or would disguise. But secret slanders cannot be disarmed, because they are secret."

Admissibility and Weight. This letter was written several years after the Callender articles, by the party charged. It must be taken as a denial of the accusations in the articles as Jefferson never admitted or acknowledged their validity, and is here saying he would not disguise the truth.

e. Letter from Jefferson to George Logan, June 20, 1816. Logan had released some of Jefferson's correspondence that Jefferson had written to him, which caused a new flurry of attacks on Jefferson:[21]

> "As to federal slanders, I never wished them to be answered, but by the tenor of my life, half a century of which has been on a theater at which the public have been spectators and competent judges of its merit. Their approbation has taught a lesson, useful to the world, that the man who fears no truths has nothing to fear from lies. I should have fancied myself half guilty had I condescended to put pen to paper in refutation of their falsehoods, or drawn to them respect by any notice from myself."

Admissibility and Weight. Written about the midpoint of his retirement from public life, it was prompted by political criticism, but sounds again the consistent theme of Jefferson's "repugnance to take any part in public discussions" to respond to the charges made against him.

Interview of Madison Hemings. A son of Sally Hemings, born in 1805, he was freed by Jefferson's will in 1826. His racial mix is not known, but he married a black woman and lived as a black.

Area of Testimony. He claimed in an interview in 1873 that Thomas Jefferson was his father. There is no record of his exact words, only as they were represented in a newspaper article in the *Pike County (Ohio) Republican* edition of March 13, 1873, by the reporter who interviewed him at that time. He stated that all the children of his mother had the same father. He is also the source of the "treaty legend" that Jefferson made a treaty with Sally to free her children.[22]

> "Soon after their arrival [from Paris], she gave birth to a child, of whom Thomas Jefferson was the father. It lived but a short time. She gave birth to four others, and Jefferson was the father of all of them. Their names were Beverly, Harriet, Madison (myself), and Eston—three sons and one daughter. We all became free agreeably to the treaty entered into by our parents before we were born."

Admissibility and Weight. This statement has been euphemistically termed "memoirs" or "reminiscences." They are not Madison's words, but the result of an interview with Samuel Wetmore which became a newspaper article. Wetmore was a printer or newspaperman by trade. He became a census taker in the 1870 Census in Ohio, and in 1873 founded the newspaper, the *Pike County Republican* in southern Ohio. He published a series of remembrances of former slaves who were living in the area. The series was entitled, "Life Among the Lowly" (a phrase created by Harriet Beecher Stowe as the subtitle to her book, *Uncle Tom's Cabin*). The article does not pretend to be a record of Hemings' exact words and contains no quotes. There is no evidence that Madison ever read the article and adopted it as his "memoirs." He acknowledged that his information on the paternity issue was told to him, since he was born in 1805, as the sixth child, and would have no personal knowledge of the events leading to the births of the first five, and would only have been three years old when the youngest child, Eston, was born in 1808. This is the first mention of a "treaty" between Sally Hemings and Jefferson.[23] Madison Hemings cannot attest to the truth of his statement, so this is double hearsay, and would not be admissible. There is no basis on which to assert that Sally Hemings is the source of his information. It is not admissible under the Pedigree Rule, because it cannot be established that the statement in the article was adopted by him or by any other family members. The Pedigree Rule exception to hearsay does not apply if better evidence is available, so DNA tests would have to be conducted on the remains of Madison's son, William Hemings, as a negative test would rule out a Jefferson paternity for the Madison Hemings descendants.[24]

Journal of John Hartwell Cocke. He was acquainted with Jefferson and implied in his journal in January 1853 that Jefferson had illegitimate slave children. He wrote in his journal again in April 1859 that bachelors kept slave women as substitutes for wives and cited Jefferson as an example.[25]

a. January 26, 1853:

> "The Reverend Lemuel Hatch of No. Carolina informed me, that two wealthy friends of his of the old No State has lately each sent away from their premises a slave woman with quite a large number of children the illegitimate [spawn?] of the Institution. Begotten in social contract with their lawful wives and white children...I can enumerate a score of such cases in our beloved Ant. Dominion that have come my way thro' life, without seeking for them—were they enumerated with the statistics of the state—they would be found by the hundreds—nor is it to be wondered at, when Mr. Jeffersons notorious example is considered."

Admissibility and Weight. The "notorious example" is open to interpretation. Did it mean Jefferson had slave children, or permitted miscegenation at Monticello? It also seems clear that his information on his first example of illegitimate slave children is hearsay ("**Hatch of No. Carolina informed...**"). His reference to the "notorious example" also seems to be the product of information or rumor and not direct knowledge ("**I can innumerate a score of such cases in our beloved Ant. Dominion that** have come in my way thro' life…"). He cites no incident of Jefferson's cohabitation with Sally Hemings. His journal in the first person is probably authentic under the ancient document rule. It would have to sustain an objection as to hearsay to be admissible.

b. April 23, 1859:

> "…all Bachelors—or large majority—at least—keep as a substitute for a wife—some individual of their our own slaves. In Virginia, this damnable practice prevails as much as anywhere—and probably more—as Mr. Jefferson's example can be [   ] for its defense."

Admissibility and Weight. Cocke was a member of the Board of Visitors at the University of Virginia and assisted Jefferson in the lottery designed to sell some of Jefferson's lands to pay off his debts. It is not known how close their relationship was. These statements are from Cocke's private diary. Cocke does not claim to have observed "Jefferson's example," and it is unclear whether he was assuming that allegations made by others half a century earlier were true. The diary is admissible as an ancient document but the entries would be objectionable on the grounds of hearsay.

Letter from Ellen Coolidge to her husband Joseph Coolidge, October 24, 1858. Ellen Coolidge was the daughter of Martha Jefferson, granddaughter of Thomas Jefferson, born in 1796, and visited and lived at Monticello.[26]

> "He lived, whenever he was at Monticello, and entirely for the last seventeen years of his life, in the midst of these young people, surrounded by them, his intercourse with them of the freest and most affectionate kind. How comes it that his immoralities were never suspected by his own family—that his daughter and her children rejected with horror and contempt the charges brought against him. That my brother, then a young man certain to know all that was going on behind the scenes, positively declares his indignant disbelief in the imputations and solemnly affirms that he never saw or heard the smallest thing which could lead him to suspect that his grandfather's life was other than perfectly pure. His apartments had no private entrance not perfectly accessible and visible to all

the household. No female domestic ever entered his chambers except at hours when he was known not to be there and none could have entered without being exposed to the public gaze…

"One woman known to Mr. J. Q. Adams and others as "dusky Sally" was pretty notoriously the mistress of a married man, a near relation of Mr. Jefferson's, and there can be small question that her children were his. They were all fair and all set free at my grandfather's death, or had been suffered to absent themself permanently before he died."

Admissibility and Weight. Her comments on the layout of Monticello would be admissible. Her references to her brother's "indignant belief" and his confiding in her the comments of Peter Carr would be hearsay. It is unclear whether she had personal knowledge that Sally Hemings was **"notoriously the mistress of a married man, a near relation of Mr. Jefferson's…"** and that comment would not be admissible. Cohabitation is a crucial element in this claim and her personal observation that no "domestic" entered Jefferson's chambers would be admissible.

Letter from Henry S. Randall to James Parton, June 1, 1868. Randall had written *Life of Jefferson* in 1858, and it is assumed this interview with Thomas Jefferson Randolph was prior to that work. James Parton used some of the information in the letter in his *The Life of Thomas Jefferson* in 1874.[27]

"Col. Randolph informed me that there was not the shadow of suspicion that Mr. Jefferson in this or any other instance had commerce with female slaves. At the periods when these Carr children were born, he, Col. Randolph, had charge of Monticello. He gave all the general directions, gave out their clothes to the slaves, etc. etc. He said Sally Hening (sic) was treated, dressed, etc., exactly like the rest. He said Mr. Jefferson never locked the door of his room by day: and that he (Col. Randolph) slept within sound of his breathing at night. He said he had never seen a motion, or a look, or a circumstance which led him to suspect for an instant that there was a particle more of familiarity between Mr. Jefferson and Sally Henings than between him and the most repulsive servant in the establishment…"

Admissibility and Weight. The excerpt quoted from the Randall letter was written about ten years after the conversation between Randall and Randolph. The letter is hearsay and it would not be admissible. The passage in the letter that Sally Hemings **"had children which resembled Mr. Jefferson so closely that it was plain that they had his blood in their veins..."** is often quoted out of context as evidence of Jefferson's possible paternity. The clear position of Randolph is that **"there was not the shadow of suspicion..."** of a Jefferson-slave relationship.

Interview of Edmund Bacon. Bacon was an overseer at Monticello beginning about 1806 before Sally Hemings' last child was born.[28]

> "He freed one girl some years before he died, and there was a great deal of talk about it. She was nearly as white as anybody and very beautiful. People said he freed her because she was his own daughter. She was not his daughter; she was _____'s daughter. I know that. I have seen him come out of her mother's room many a morning when I went up to Monticello very early."

Admissibility and Weight. Bacon gave this interview in 1862. His chronology appears faulty as Harriet (the girl referred to) was born about five years before Bacon came to Monticello. It is possible that Bacon worked at Monticello before he became overseer in 1806, and would have known that Sally Hemings had a lover. The original manuscript has been lost and there are objections to authenticity unless the copy now extant can be proved to be a true copy of the original. The interview would be hearsay unless Bacon read it and adopted it as his words.

Interview of Israel Jefferson. Israel Jefferson was born at Monticello.[29]

> "I also know that his servant, Sally Hemings, (mother to my old friend and former companion at Monticello, Madison Hemings), was employed as a chamber-maid, and that Mr. Jefferson was on the most intimate terms; that, in fact, she was his concubine. This I know from my intimacy with both parties, and when Madison Hemings declares he is a natural son of Thomas Jefferson, the author of the Declaration of Independence, and that his brothers Beverly and Eston and sister Harriet are of the same parentage, I can as conscientiously confirm his statement as any other fact which I believe from circumstances but do not positively know."

Admissibility and Weight. This interview was published in the *Pike County (Ohio) Republican,* December 25, 1873, as part of the Wetmore series. Israel Jefferson was seventy-six years old and relates incidents that took place before he was eight years old (he was eight years old at the time of Eston Hemings' birth). He could not have known that Jefferson was on "intimate terms" with Sally Hemings from his own "intimacy with both parties..." There are no quotes or any device to indicate these are Israel's words. There is no proof he ever read this article or adopted the words as his own. This interview is hearsay and inadmissible.

Letter of Thomas Jefferson Randolph to the *Pike County (Ohio) Republican, c.* 1874. Thomas Jefferson Randolph was the grandson of Thomas Jefferson and lived many years at Monticello. He was manager at Monticello in the last ten years of Jefferson's life and one of the principal Executors of his will.[30]

> "He is thus made to recollect distinctly events occurring a month before his birth...
>
> "Israel was never employed in any post of trust or confidence about the house at Monticello...
>
> "To my own knowledge and that of others 60 years ago the paternity of these parties were admitted by others."

Admissibility and Weight. This letter was written by Randolph as a reply to the statements attributed to Israel Jefferson in the *Pike County Republican.* He points out that Israel remembered the departure of Jefferson for Washington to assume the duties of President in 1800, before Israel was born. His comments demonstrate that Israel Jefferson's memory was either faulty or he was dependent on information told him by others. The importance of the letter is the denial of Jefferson's paternity. Randolph's letter would be admissible.

Jefferson's Farm Records. Jefferson kept accounts and records in a farm book, account book, and garden book. These show the births and deaths of both his family and his slave family, as well as the times he left and returned to Monticello.

Admissibility and Weight. These books have been edited and qualify both as ancient documents and records kept in the regular course of business. They are generally accepted as authentic records of Jefferson and are admissible.

Expert Testimony

The DNA tests. DNA tests on five male line descendants of two sons of Thomas Jefferson's paternal uncle, Field Jefferson, and five male line descendants of two sons of Thomas Woodson, and one male line descendant of Eston Hemings, and three male line descendants of three sons of John Carr (grandfather of Samuel and Peter Carr) were conducted by Eugene A. Foster as reported in the November 5, 1998, issue of *Nature.* There was a subsequent test on another Woodson male line descendant.

Area of Testimony. The expert who performed the DNA tests would be allowed to testify to the results. It cannot be determined whether the methodology used in conducting the tests would survive a challenge. The tests were conducted by Foster without any independent controls. There is no explanation of how the samples were taken to England for testing, and it does not appear that the results were subject to any peer review. It is not known what information was provided to the experts questioned by the Research Committee whose responses were recorded in the Committee Report.

a. The tests do not support the paternity of Thomas Jefferson for the claimant Thomas Woodson.
b. There are no tests to establish a DNA match for the claimants Beverly, Harriet, or Madison.
c. There is a match for the claimant Eston Hemings. His Y chromosome haplotype is identical to the male line descendants of Field Jefferson.
d. There is no match between any of the claimants and Samuel or Peter Carr.

Admissibility and Weight. The DNA tests would have to pass a rigorous cross examination before they could be admitted. If admitted, the weight to be given to them would be accorded by the trier of fact. Jefferson's Farm Book may establish his presence at Monticello during each of Sally

Hemings' conceptions, but it does not establish Sally's presence. There is no evidence of access to her, so the DNA can establish nothing more than the statistical possibility of the paternity of Eston Hemings.

William and Mary Quarterly, **January 2000: The Coincidence of Sally Hemings' Conceptions.** Jefferson's Farm Book provides the dates that he was at Monticello, and it appears he was present in the nine month period prior to each of the births of Sally Hemings' children.

Area of Testimony. This study by Frazier D. Neiman of the statistical relationship between Thomas Jefferson's visits to Monticello and Sally Hemings' conceptions was to establish a probability that only Thomas Jefferson could be the father.

Admissibility and Weight. The problem with the study is acknowledged by Neiman. The study no more establishes the probability of Jefferson being the father of Sally Hemings' children, than it does of any other children born at Monticello within the nine month period after his visits and would not be admissible. The evidence of Jefferson's presence at Monticello is circumstantial evidence of paternity and admissible, but it must be supported by evidence of cohabitation between Jefferson and Sally Hemings. The Farm Book and other records must also establish that Sally Hemings was present at Monticello during her periods of conception for each of the six children. There are too many factors that must be assumed or are unknown to support expert testimony on the "odds" of paternity.

Summary of the Evidence of Jefferson's Paternity of the Hemings Children

There is no burden on Jefferson descendants to disprove the claimed paternity. The burden of proof is on those who claim paternity. The standard is clear and convincing evidence.

The "proximity argument" must be examined. The records kept by Thomas Jefferson may demonstrate that he was present at Monticello at the times that Sally Hemings conceived. There also must be a methodology to establish that Sally Hemings was there at the same time.

Cohabitation must be proved. There is no contemporaneous statement by the daughters and grandchildren who occupied Monticello, by

Jefferson's brother, sister, nephews, or other assorted relatives who visited Monticello, or by the numerous visitors, that contact of an intimate or personal nature occurred between Jefferson and Hemings, an event that could not have escaped their scrutiny.[31] Ellen Coolidge, a granddaughter of Jefferson who visited and lived at Monticello, denies any such conduct. Although Sally Hemings lived at Monticello for 36 years, there is not a scintilla of proof of any intimate conduct between her and Jefferson, or any demonstrations of affection or commerce of any kind. Presence is not equivalent to cohabitation. Inferences that Jefferson had intercourse merely because he was the master and Hemings was a slave may not be drawn without some proof of a physical relationship.

The claim must originate from the mother. The Madison Hemings interview does not claim his mother told him Jefferson was the father of her children. He had to have been told by someone of these events which occurred before his birth, so these claims in the newspaper article are hearsay. There is no such claim by his sister Harriet or his two brothers, Beverly or Eston. There is no other source to support Madison that Sally Hemings made such a claim. If Sally had been Jefferson's "concubine," and had borne him six children over a period of thirteen years, her status at Monticello would have been unique and known. She lived for eight years as a free woman. No one in the entire thirty-six year span of her time at Monticello reports a claim by her that Jefferson was the father of any of her children.

Sally Hemings' family did not claim Jefferson paternity. Two brothers of Sally Hemings, James and Robert, were freed by Jefferson in the 1790s.[32] James was with Jefferson when Sally arrived in Paris at the age of fourteen and would have observed their relationship. He returned from Paris with Jefferson and Sally at the time she would have been pregnant with Tom Woodson. He was freed by Jefferson in 1796 and lived until 1801, and during that time never accused Jefferson of fathering any of the four children of Sally Hemings, who were born prior to his own death. Another brother, John, was freed by Jefferson's will, as were two of Betty Hemings' grandsons, Joe Fossett and Burwell. There is no record that any of them claimed Jefferson was the father of any of the children of Sally Hemings.

149

Oral history is not evidence. The Woodson family has maintained an oral history that their ancestor was the Tom born to Sally Hemings after her return from Paris. Recent DNA evidence indicates that their ancestor was not the son of Thomas Jefferson. The fallacy in the Woodson oral history demonstrates the reason that oral history is not evidence and not admissible. The oral history of the Madison Hemings family that Jefferson was father to Sally's children cannot rise higher than the evidence available from the participants and witnesses at the time the children were born. There is no original source for their belief other than the Callender articles. The Eston Hemings family had a tradition they were descended from a Jefferson relative and are now in the unlikely situation of "revising" their oral history.

The "single father postulate" is a product of the imagination. The claim that Sally's children had a single father based on the "closeness of the family" as established by her children naming their children after their siblings, is a postulate unsupported by any empirical studies. It is an opinion which could only be advanced through expert testimony, which had been reached by the expert through the evaluation of data and information. No study or expert has been identified that supports such a view.

No factual basis can be shown for the "resemblance claim." The claim that the children of Sally Hemings bore a likeness to Jefferson started with the Callender article of December 8, 1802, referring to Tom Woodson, who, if he did exist, had no Jefferson blood. Later, a letter from Henry Randall to the Jefferson biographer James Parton alleged that his source was Jefferson's grandson, Thomas Jefferson Randolph. This letter was written in 1868, ten years after the conversation, in which Randall has Randolph say **"she had children which resembled Mr. Jefferson,"** and that a dinner guest was **"startled"** at the resemblance of a servant. The children who resembled Jefferson are not identified, nor is the one who "startled" the guest, but the point of Randolph's observation is to deny Jefferson is the father. Moreover, the letter is hearsay and inadmissible. Anecdotal stories that Eston bore a "likeness" to a statue of Jefferson are not evidence, but rather stories that have become part of local lore. A slave who looked like Jefferson would have been the most startling circumstance at Monticello, but not a single record survives contemporary with the years the Hemingses lived at Monticello that asserted any of them had a likeness to Jefferson.

The age difference and strange birth pattern. Jefferson's wife died in 1782. There is no evidence that his affair with Maria Cosway in France was sexual. After his return to the U.S. in 1789 there is no evidence of any sexual liaisons. If the claimed relationship of Hemings and Jefferson started in Paris, it was strangely barren for five years, although clearly, Hemings was fecund, producing a child in 1795 and five more over the next 13 years, an average of one every two years. Jefferson had six children by his wife in a ten year marriage. Jefferson would have started this relationship when he was 52, his age at the first birth, and continued until he was 65, his age at the last. It is likely expert medical testimony would characterize sexual activity at this age as statistically low. The children were born while Jefferson was one of the best known figures in the country, vice-president from 1796 to 1800 and president from 1801 to 1809.[33] Once he returned to Monticello to stay, following his second term, the births stopped, when Sally Hemings was 35.

No source exists for the "treaty legend." According to this story, although Sally could remain free in France, she agreed to return from Paris upon Jefferson's promise that he would free her future children when they reached 21 years. Jefferson did grant freedom in his will[34] to Madison and Eston, Sally Hemings' two youngest sons, when they reached 21. Jefferson had previously recorded in his Farm Book that the two other children, Beverly and Harriet, had "run away." Ellen Coolidge thought they were allowed to leave because they were able to pass into white society. The claim that Jefferson assisted Harriet to leave comes from the Edmund Bacon interview which is hearsay and inadmissible. The origin of the "treaty legend" between Jefferson and Sally Hemings to free her children is the 1873 interview of Madison Hemings which is hearsay and inadmissible. The favored treatment of the Hemings family appears more to relate to Betty Hemings rather than Sally, as Jefferson let two of Betty's sons go in the 1790s, and freed another, plus four of her grandsons (two were Sally's children) in his will.[35] The status of the Hemingses as household servants and artisans—rather than field hands—began when Sally was a small child.

Historical Evaluation of Jefferson Paternity

Influenced by the 1974 Brodie book (Fawn Brodie, *Thomas Jefferson: An Intimate History*), there have been three significant evaluations of the historical evidence which have concluded that Jefferson's paternity of the Hemings children was likely.[36]

It is not the purpose of this analysis to argue the issue on the basis of the methodology used in those evaluations. These are some brief observations on their conclusions tested against a legal evidentiary standard.

Thomas Jefferson and Sally Hemings: An American Controversy. Annette Gordon-Reed, 1997. This book by a lawyer recognized the legal insufficiency of the evidence, and used an historical approach in the form of a lawyer's brief. This permitted her to compile all the evidence, whether or not legally admissible, in an argument that Jefferson's paternity, while not proved, was plausible. She acknowledges in the updated printing that "the DNA test does not prove that the descendant of Eston Hemings was a direct descendant of Thomas Jefferson."

Her thesis of paternity relies heavily on the Madison Hemings "memoirs" which she mistakenly terms "direct evidence," and on the Callender articles, which she believes have enough correct details to show that Callender was picking up on believable gossip.

She accepts the validity of the "resemblance claim," and never questions why such a dramatic circumstance is not mentioned for forty-five years, and only then by Jefferson's grandson, Thomas Jefferson Randolph, who supposedly has related in confidence this information, which would have been obvious to the hundreds of persons who passed through Monticello. She is no more critical of the number of times that the canard passed from mouth to mouth that Eston Hemings resembled Jefferson before it found its way some seventy years later into the *Daily Scioto Gazette* in 1902.

Journal *Nature:* "Jefferson Fathered Slave's Last Child," November 5, 1998. This issue featured the DNA results that showed Thomas Jefferson had the same haplotype as descendants of Eston Hemings.[37] The magazine overreached with its headline which relied on what another article in that issue of *Nature* termed "three pieces of evidence," the "resemblance claim," the Madison Hemings "memoirs," and the "proximity argument."

This revisionist analysis in the same issue by Eric Lander and Joseph Ellis was triggered by the DNA tests. Ellis, in his book *American Sphinx,* denied the Jefferson paternity and acknowledged that so did most of the "Jefferson specialists." Why these three items of evidence suddenly became persuasive of paternity after the DNA test results is unclear. The analysis does not pretend, as Gordon-Reed did, to be a "legal" review, and the methodology and standard of proof followed by Lander and Ellis is not explained.

Thomas Jefferson Memorial Foundation Report of the Research Committee on Thomas Jefferson and Sally Hemings.[38]

Methodology. The Report indicates that the Research Committee did not have a test which it applied evenly to all the available information. In some cases it argued away or failed to acknowledge Jefferson's denials in various letters, while at the same time placing extraordinary reliance on a reporter's version of what Madison Hemings said he was told about his paternity. The lack of controls or methodology to weigh the information is contrary to Dan Jordan's statement following the Committee Report that his appointed staff committee evaluated the scientific results and other relative evidence "in a systematic and comprehensive way . . . " He does not point out any such system for evaluation of the evidence, nor does the Committee appear to follow a deductive approach to its result but, in fact, manipulates the evidentiary sources.[39]

Standard of Proof. a. "Strong Likelihood." This is the comment of Daniel P. Jordan, President of the Foundation, in his statement which was released concurrent with the Committee Report. This is neither a legal term nor a term of art, so it is not possible to know how this test is applied. It appears to be a subjective test that the conclusion is satisfactory to Dr. Jordan.

b. "High Probability and Most Likely." The Report concludes that the "currently available documentary and statistical evidence, indicates a high probability that Thomas Jefferson fathered Eston Hemings, and that he was most likely the father of all six of Sally Hemings' children…" Like the "strong likelihood" of Jordan's comment, this is a subjective test applied by the committee.

New Conclusion. The Committee Report appears to follow the same thematic formula employed by Gordon-Reed to marshal support for Jefferson's paternity. Other than the DNA tests, it does not present new information, and relies on "birth pattern," the Madison Hemings "memoirs," the "resemblance claim," the "proximity argument," and surprisingly, the "oral history" of the Woodson and Hemings families. The Report uncovers nothing new, but makes the same reversal from the former position of the Monticello staff on the probability of Jefferson's paternity as did the Lander-Ellis analysis.

The "Single Father Postulate." This postulate was devised by the Committee to extend the DNA test results to all the Hemings children. Since the DNA tests eliminated the legendary Tom Woodson, and only matched Eston to the Jefferson haplotype, the Committee adjusted its sights. While sympathetic to the "oral history" of the Woodson family, the Committee eliminated Tom as a prospective son. It then concluded that the remaining Hemings siblings had a "closeness" that could only come from a single father. Since Jefferson was present during Sally's conceptions, and Eston had the Jefferson haplotype, the Committee concluded that Jefferson must be his father; and since they all had the same father, it assumed that Jefferson was the father of them all. The "closeness" is supposedly demonstrated by siblings naming their children after each other. This is a dubious assertion, complicated by name manipulation. The Report ignores the lack of any evidence of cohabitation or access by Jefferson to Hemings, nor does it cite any statistical or empirical support for the closeness syndrome that justifies the single father postulate.

Conclusion

Under Virginia law, unless there is an admission of paternity by the father, a claim must be pursued under the statutory procedure. Evidence to establish paternity means oral testimony or documents that pass the legal test of admissibility. The case against Thomas Jefferson is devoid of admissible evidence.

There is no direct evidence from any source during Jefferson's life that he was the father of any of the children born to Sally Hemings between 1790 and 1808. Although Jefferson may have been present at Monticello during each of Sally's conceptions, there is no proof that she was at Monticello during these periods. There is also not a scintilla of proof of any cohabitation or physical intimacy between Jefferson and Hemings during the approximately thirty-seven years she resided at Monticello after her return from Paris until Jefferson's death.

The two prominent documents written long after Jefferson's death and relied on as paternity evidence are hearsay and inadmissible. These are the 1868 Parton letter, which seemed to raise within the family a "resemblance claim" against Jefferson, and the 1873 Madison Hemings interview which created the "treaty legend."[40]

The 1998 DNA test results identify a chromosomal link between Eston Hemings and the male Jefferson line. Thomas Jefferson is included among the twenty-five possible fathers, but he is eliminated because of the lack of admissible evidence. The unproved single father postulate is a device that substitutes imagination for hard evidence.

It is surprising that the sources and the nature of the information that make up the "Tom and Sally Myth" in the Committee Report has put the academic community into such a quandary. It is a tale which should return to its status as no more than a footnote to the Jefferson legacy, based on unproved allegations and fueled by the imagination.

Endnotes

1. All references to statutes are from the current Virginia Code.

2. *Washington Federalist*, article of June 19, 1805, *Callender, Jefferson and the Sally Story: The Scandalmonger and the Newspaper Wars of 1802*, Rebecca McMurry and James F. McMurry, Jr., Old Virginia Books, Edinburg, VA, 2000, pp. 65–67. An 1847 interview with a former Monticello slave has Isaac Jefferson repeating the rumor that, "folks said that these Hemings were old Mr. Wayles children." *Jefferson at Monticello*, James A. Bear, Jr., The University of Virginia Press (1967), p. 4.

3. *Thomas Jefferson: An Intimate History,* Fawn M. Brodie, W. W. Norton & Co. (1974), pp. 447–482.

4. See *Report on Thomas Jefferson and Sally Hemings,* Thomas Jefferson Memorial Foundation Research Committee, 2000, Appendix ., p. 1 (hereafter, as Committee Report).

5. Sally Hemings is an historical cipher. There are some physical descriptions of her, but even in the 1873 interview, the reporter does not relate any statements by Madison Hemings describing his mother's personal characteristics. In fact, information about her is so slight, one would conclude she was a person of no importance at Monticello.

6. The only source of the Callender articles in typescript is the booklet by Rebecca L. McMurry and James F. McMurry, *Callender, Jefferson and the Sally Story—The Scandalmonger and The Newspaper War of 1802,* Old Virginia Books, Edinburg, VA, 2000. It also contains an excellent short biography of Callender. The articles may be downloaded from http://home.earthlink.net/~oldvabooks/.

7. *Richmond Recorder,* article of September 1, 1802, *Callender, Jefferson and the Sally Story: The Scandalmonger and the Newspaper Wars of 1802,* pp. 12–13.

8. *Richmond Recorder,* article of September 22, 1802, *Callender, Jefferson and the Sally Story: The Scandalmonger and the Newspaper Wars of 1802,* pp. 36–37.

9. *Richmond Recorder,* article of November 10, 1802, *Callender, Jefferson and the Sally Story: The Scandalmonger and the Newspaper Wars of 1802,* p. 48.

10. *Richmond Recorder,* article of December 8, 1802, *Callender, Jefferson and the Sally Story: The Scandalmonger and the Newspaper Wars of 1802,* pp. 55–56.

11. *Thomas Jefferson: An Intimate History,* p. 323.

12. The lineage is based on the 1805 Thomas Turner claim that John Wayles was Sally Hemings' father, and that her mother, Betty Hemings, was half-white. Under Virginia law at the time, one with 1/8 Negro blood was legally white (Revised Code of 1819, c.111 §11).

13. *Jefferson at Monticello, Recollections of Edmund Bacon,* Hamilton

Wilcox Pierson, edited by James A. Bear, University Press of Virginia (1967), pp. 102–103.

14. This reference to an event some sixty years old, the source long obscured, was cited as "unquestioned" evidence in the Committee Report. (Committee Report Appendix F, p. 1) The article is noteworthy, however, because it purports to quote Eston who does not claim Jefferson parentage. *Thomas Jefferson and Sally Hemings: An American Controversy,* Annette Gordon-Reed, University Press of Virginia (1997), p. 15.

15. The Woodson family has an "oral history" of a Jefferson ancestry. Although the recent DNA test was conclusive that no Jefferson was the father of Tom, many of them press on in their belief. According to the Madison Hemings interview, Sally arrived at Monticello pregnant, but the child "lived but a short time." Whether Callender was given information by someone, or whether he made it up is not known, so he remains the only source for the mysterious Tom. See *Fame and the Founding Fathers,* Douglas Adair, Institute for Early American History and Culture, Williamsburg, Chapter VIII.

16. References to the number of Sally's children can be confusing. She had six births recorded at Monticello. Two died in infancy, including the doubtful 1799 child, and four, Beverly, Harriet, Madison, and Eston, survived to adulthood. If Tom existed, he would have been the first birth, for a total of seven children.

17. See letter from Thomas Jefferson to Judge John Tyler, June 28, 1804, *Thomas Jefferson, Writings,* Merrill D. Peterson, Library of America (1984), p. 1146.

18. See letter from Thomas Jefferson to James Sullivan, May 21, 1805, *The Works of Thomas Jefferson,* edited by Paul Leicester Ford. The attacks on Jefferson in the northeast are discussed in *Jefferson the President: Second Term,* Dumas Malone, Little, Brown & Company (1974), pp. 11–17.

19. Because Hemings is not named, some have argued that the charges involving her are not included in Jefferson's denial. A review of the June 19, 1805, issue of the *Washington Federalist* reveals the letter from Thomas Turner which repeats the Callender charges, so this was again at issue during the furor over the Walker Affair.

20. See letter from Thomas Jefferson to William Duane, March 22, 1806, *The Works of Thomas Jefferson,* edited by Paul Leicester Ford. For a description of the controversy that preceded this letter, see *Jefferson and His Time: The Sage of Monticello,* Dumas Malone, Little, Brown & Co., (1981), pp. 114–117.

21. See letter from Thomas Jefferson to George Logan, June 28, 1816, *The Works of Thomas Jefferson,* edited by Paul Leicester Ford.

22. *Thomas Jefferson: An Intimate History,* pp. 471–476.

23. The treaty legend is unsupported. Those who accept it stumble badly when they try to explain why Sally Hemings, pregnant with Tom, and knowing she could stay in France as a free woman, returned to the U.S. on the promise her future children would grow up as slaves, but be freed at their adulthood. She lived all but the last few years of her life as a slave at Monticello.

24. For those who wish to prove a Jefferson paternity, there is no case unless this interview can be portrayed as more than an unsupported belief by Madison Hemings. To that end, Annette Gordon-Reed calls them "memoirs," to Fawn Brodie they are "reminiscences," and the Committee Report implies it constitutes "testimony" of Sally Hemings. (Committee Report Appendix F, p. 2)

25. See Journal of John Hartwell Cocke, January 26, 1853, and April 23, 1859, original University of Virginia Library, with typescript of extract, *Report on Thomas Jefferson and Sally Hemings,* Thomas Jefferson Memorial Foundation Research Committee, 2000.

26. Ellen Coolidge was two years older than Beverly Hemings and would have grown up with her 11 brothers and sisters and the Hemings children. Madison Hemings supposedly was able to name them in his interview in 1873. They were often at Monticello and a relationship between Thomas Jefferson and Sally Hemings could not have escaped the scrutiny of Jefferson's grandchildren. See letter from Ellen Coolidge in Annette Gordon-Reed, *Thomas Jefferson and Sally Hemings: An American Controversy* (Charlottesville, 1997), pp. 258–260 and *Life of Jefferson,* Henry Randall, New York (1858), pp. 342–344. See also Appendix to this book. For a family memoir, printed in 1871 by a great granddaugh-

ter, see *The Domestic Life of Thomas Jefferson,* Sarah N. Randolph, University Press of Virginia (1978).

27. It would have been possible for Parton, dubbed the "Father of Modern Biography," to have corresponded directly with Randolph at the time of the Randall letter. It is not known why he did not verify Randall's account. The entire letter was later printed in a biography of Parton. See *James Parton: The Father of Modern Biography,* Milton E. Flower, Durham (1951), pp. 236–239.

28. Bacon was interviewed in Kentucky, where he was then living, by the Reverend Hamilton W. Pierson. *Jefferson at Monticello, Recollections of Edmund Bacon,* Hamilton Wilcox Pierson, edited by James A. Bear, University Press of Virginia (1967), pp. 102–103.

29. *Thomas Jefferson: An Intimate History,* pp. 447–482.

30. This letter was probably never sent. See letter of Jefferson's grandson Thomas Jefferson Randolph to editor of *Pike County Republican,* undated, original University of Virginia Library, Accession Number 8937 with typescript version, *Report on Thomas Jefferson and Sally Hemings,* Thomas Jefferson Memorial Foundation Research Committee, 2000.

31. The law does not conclude because there is no evidence that all participated in a grand conspiracy of silence. Of equal significance, and ignored by the Committee Report, was Jefferson's constant entreaties to his daughters to live, if not at Monticello, then close by. There is no evidence that they were aware their father was also the father of Sally Hemings' children. The only conclusion, based on the evidence, is that the liaison did not exist, and their family closeness was without hypocrisy.

32. Robert could read and write and was allowed to move around much as a free man even before manumission by Jefferson in 1795. He never raised a claim that his sister Sally was Jefferson's mistress.

33. The last two children were born in 1805 and 1808, during Jefferson's second term as President, in the face of the uproar that Callender's articles elicited in 1802. Jefferson supposedly risked his presidency and his reputation to be with Sally Hemings, yet never showed the slightest sign of affection for her and the children they produced.

34. See Will of Thomas Jefferson in the Appendix.

35. Jefferson's financial situation would have prevented his freeing his slaves under Virginia law. It may also be that he would have let more or all go but for the legal claim of his creditors. See Revised Code of 1819, c.111, §§53–54. Also, under Virginia law, he remained responsible for them, so keeping them at Monticello may have been the only option. Jefferson expressed to the end of life concern for freed slaves who had no means of support. Those who decry Jefferson as a "slaveholder"do not offer a solution to the then current laws and social conditions if he had freed them all.

36. Fawn Brodie produced a book that was excellent in the details of her research but flawed in her manipulation of the evidence in which she claims possibilities as historical fact. *Thomas Jefferson: An Intimate History*, Fawn Brodie, W. W. Norton & Co. (1974). For a rebuttal to her techniques, see *The Jefferson Scandals*, Virginius Dabney, Dodd, Mead & Co., 1981.

37. There were 25 males who could have fathered Eston Hemings, and eight were in the vicinity of Monticello during Sally's various pregnancies. See the chart by James Renwick Manship, *Jefferson Adult Near Relatives and DNA Linkage Study*.

38. The Report may be downloaded from http://www.monticello.org/plantation/hemings_report.html. Special attention should be given to the Minority Report. See also, *Research Report on the Jefferson-Hemings Controversy, A Critical Analysis*, by Eyler Robert Coates at http://www.angelfire.com/va/TJTruth.

39. The most disturbing aspect of the Committee Report is an obvious bias toward a desired result. An example is the selective reference to Callender's comments on James Madison, who clearly denied the Sally story, but is made to appear in the Committee Report as "acquainted with it." See *Richmond Recorder*, article of September 29, 1802, *Callender, Jefferson and the Sally Story: The Scandalmonger and the Newspaper Wars of 1802*. Fawn Brodie and Annette Gordon-Reed were advancing a thesis, but the Thomas Jefferson Memorial Foundation, known by its ownership of Monticello, claimed to be guided by independent scholarship. The Committee had no independent scholars and the report was written by a staff historian at Monticello.

40. These two documents demonstrate the purpose of the hearsay rule. In the Madison Hemings interview, he relates that Jefferson was the father of all of the Hemings children and that he made a "treaty" with Sally Hemings to free them. Madison cannot know whether this claim is true, but would have received this information from someone else. He does not relate when he was told or by whom. Yet, advocates of Jefferson's paternity continue to argue that this interview is evidence. The Randall letter claims its source is Thomas Jefferson Randolph and it sets off in quotes Randolph's words. The statements in the letter remain those of the writer, who cannot attest to the truth of any of them—only Randolph could do that. The device of the historian, certainly carried to the extreme by the proponents of a Jefferson-Hemings relationship, is to selectively extract from the documents. In doing so, not only is the hearsay rule ignored, there is no other methodology to provide a guide for determining truth from fiction except the subjective judgment of the reader.

The nation's memorial to Thomas Jefferson, third President and author of the Declaration of Independence, located in Washington, DC. The memorial was dedicated on Jefferson's 200th birthday April 13, 1943, by President Franklin Delano Roosevelt as an expression of the American people's high esteem for one of the greatest of the Founding Fathers. The domed and colonnaded memorial is reminiscent of the design Jefferson provided for his home, Monticello, and the rotunda of the University of Virginia. The walls of the memorial which surround a nineteen-foot-high statue of Jefferson bear excerpts from the two documents for which he most wanted to be remembered, the Declaration of Independence and the Virginia Statute for Religious Freedom.

Conclusion and Consequences

Bahman Batmanghelidj

What we are faced with in this Jefferson-Hemings controversy is not just a question of the sufficiency of the evidence, though it is certainly that. It is not even just a question of the proper interpretation of the evidence, though it is that also. What makes this controversy such a travesty of investigative scholarship is the manner in which insufficient evidence was manipulated, and the way much of the evidence that would exonerate Mr. Jefferson was casually disregarded or suppressed. What we see is a deliberate and unforgivable attempt to destroy the reputation of one of this great nation's greatest Founding Fathers. And what makes this crime against our heritage the more reprehensible is that it was endorsed by the long-established institution that was founded to memorialize this man who is our most brilliant Founding Father, who is without question our greatest spokesman for American democracy.

Our opposition to this travesty, therefore, is not based on a mere difference of opinion or point of view, a mere interpretation of historical events. It is based on a profound difference of principle. We cannot

163

compromise with those who seek to destroy the character of Thomas Jefferson. This is not a matter of scholarship, but of the spreading of destructive propaganda. It is not a matter of evidence, but of dissimulation. It is not a matter of interpretation, but of selecting evidence for a predetermined finding. The deliberate attempt to shape the outcome of an investigation is appalling. The lack of fairness and even-handedness is shocking. The betrayal of human greatness is revolting. And we betray our own sense of decency and self-respect by suggesting it is in any manner otherwise.

We are accused of opposing this denigration of Jefferson for "misguided personal reasons," and not because we sincerely believe the Thomas Jefferson Memorial Foundation Research Report is flawed. What misguided personal reasons? Let a fair-minded public consider all the evidence and our explanations, and then decide which of us honestly seeks to discover the truth.

We have been asked to do no more than reconsider the available evidence, but without regard to the reports and the interpretations that have already been issued. But that would be a fraudulent investigation! The salient feature of this whole controversy is not the evidence so much as the way in which the evidence has been used and manipulated for predetermined ends. This, indeed, is where the real story lies. This is the real scandal. It is not the weight of the evidence, but the work of the spin-masters that have produced this twisted mass of intentionally biased accusations, who have eliminated the exculpatory and reshaped the questionable. And this they have been able to do by relying upon a reputation and renown acquired over many decades of genuine service to the memory of this great man.

We have heard the call for "new evidence," but have seen no indication that a new evaluation of the evidence already available would be welcome. This is all part of a planned deception. Hidden behind this false appearance of openness to new evidence is the assumption that the interpretations already given to the old evidence are scholarly and well-founded. And that is the false premise. This call for "new evidence" is itself nothing more than deceptive propaganda. This is the manipulative way in which the previous evaluations are made to appear competent, supposedly to be accepted as landmarks of scholarship. It is an attempt to brain-wash the public into thinking that if those opposed to the Research Report do not come up with some entirely "new evidence," then that Report remains the definitive analysis. Such is the trickery behind this call for "new evidence."

What Is the Purpose of These Attacks?

In the face of all this trickery and deceit, we feel compelled to ask, What is the purpose behind these scurrilous attacks on a truly great man, attacks that are based on the flimsiest of *hearsay* evidence? Why do so many feel compelled to expend so much time and energy in such a frenzy to trash the reputation of our Founding Fathers, who were all truly great men and who engineered a momentous turning point in the history of the world when they established this new nation? What might be in store for this great nation if it in this way tramples on its heritage of freedom and self-government?

It has become unfashionable in this day to speak of one's love of country, and more fashionable to denigrate it and everything that is noble about it. Thomas Jefferson is without doubt one of the great political minds of the past millennium, and the chief intellectual founder of American self-government. We seem to live in an age pervaded by a self-destructive, tabloid mentality which has taken over, not just newspapers devoted to all kinds of sensationalism, but even highly trained academics who should know better. Every effort is made to discredit the character of the Founding Fathers, and to tear down the position they hold in the American mind. The Declaration of Independence, the greatest document in the history of human liberty, is itself denigrated in an effort to show it was nothing special and should not be accorded the reverence in which we have held it. The New Orleans School Board on October 27, 1997, voted to remove the name of George Washington, our first President, from one of its elementary schools because he was once a slave-holder, ignoring the fact that he was instrumental in establishing a nation built on the inalienable rights of human beings that has stood as a beacon of hope for blacks and every other oppressed people throughout the world.

We can only hope that, while tearing down the character and reputations of those men who established this great nation, we do not also destroy their ideas and the principles which are the foundation of this nation's greatness. But that, too, apparently is part of this campaign of denigration. The basic principles of democracy, of majority rule, of self-government, are also under attack. None of this bodes well for a nation founded on principles. Shall we replace those principles with trash ideas based on deceit and deception also? Shall out of this destructive "cultural revolution" arise greater principles of just government than are found in the writings of Thomas Jefferson? Those of us who love this country and the principles of human liberty it has stood for, and towards which it has constantly progressed, must resist these efforts to undermine and destroy the foundations that were laid in the past for the precious rights to life, liberty, and pursuit of happiness that we now enjoy.

Our efforts on behalf of Thomas Jefferson are of vital importance to his legacy and to his place in American thought and political philosophy. But Thomas Jefferson is important, not just to us in America, but to freedom-loving people throughout the world, and rightly so. His ideas and principles have inspired millions, and point the way for people of every land to enjoy "the blessings of self-government." This heritage is too great a treasure to be thrown away so casually. It is too important, not only to the future of our children and grandchildren, but to the many developing nations around the globe.

Jefferson's Legacy

It is thrilling to see whole nations of people around the world rising up and demanding self-government and the overthrow of their tyrants. But it is not enough for a people to be successful in their struggle to win their independence and their freedom from oppression. It is necessary, if a people are to remain free, that they institute a just and rightful government that will protect their inalienable rights after the freedom to establish government of the people is won. Without a proper form of government, a nation will just fall under a new oppressor and be exploited by new masters. Preventing this loss of self-government is precisely what Thomas Jefferson has to offer. His writings detail the principles of government that will allow a people to govern themselves, and to maintain checks and balances that will help assure that their nation does indeed remain free and independent, that individual rights remain protected, and that the happiness of all is fostered. Not only newly formed nations, but new immigrants coming to America and school children growing up in America need to become acquainted with these principles set forth by Jefferson, for as Abraham Lincoln said, "The principles of Jefferson are the axioms of a free society."

The Historical Treatment of Jefferson

No other American President has had so much written about him as has been written about Thomas Jefferson. Unfortunately, some of what was written is inaccurate to say the least. For example, English historian Paul Johnson, in his book, *The History of the American People*, states that Jefferson had his wife and concubine living under the same roof. But, when Jefferson's wife Martha was alive, Sally Hemings was eight-and-a-half years old! Are we then to conclude that the alleged love affair started when Sally was the age of four or five, or possibly six?

Again, at the time of the election of 1800, the opposition press—the Federalists—spread the rumor that Jefferson was an Atheist, and as was the habit of Jefferson, he did not publicly deny such charges. In his *Notes on the State of Virginia,* Jefferson wrote "Can the liberties of a nation be thought secure when we have removed their only firm basis, a conviction in the minds of the people that these liberties are of the gift of God?" thus founding his entire political philosophy on an entitlement of man that was given him by God. But the rumor that Jefferson was an Atheist still persists even today. The American Ambassador to the Court of St. James, Phillip Lader, in an otherwise acceptable speech given in London on September 23, 1999, stated that, "Jefferson probably did not believe in God." Nothing can be further from the truth!

The Foundations of a Free Society

Even though Jefferson was in France when the Constitution was written in 1787, Madison wrote to him explaining the miracle that had occurred despite all of the conflicting views and attitudes and interests of the various states. Finally, the consent of all the parties had been obtained.

But to his considerable chagrin and dismay, the letter Jefferson wrote in return did not contain the praise that he no doubt had expected. Jefferson asked him about the protection for religious freedom, about term limitations for the Chief Executive, and about a Bill of Rights for the citizens. He dismissed the idea that these guarantees were not necessary in a "limited" government. These rights had to be carved in granite, and, indeed, a Bill of Rights was made the first order of business by the new Congress as a condition for approval of the whole document.

What is so little recognized today is the key role that religious freedom plays in a free society, and the key role that Thomas Jefferson played in establishing religious freedom in America. Jefferson approached this problem, not as a provincial Virginian, concerned only with the problems of his own country, but as a person of broad perspective, acquainted with the role of religion in the life of man throughout history and around the world. If anyone goes to the Library of Congress and looks in the priceless rare book section, they will find there two copies of the Koran: one in French, and one in English. The English version has Jefferson's handwriting at the side of a number of pages indicating that he almost certainly had read the Koran. And the insight that he brought to the question of church and state resulted in the broadest concept of religious freedom, fully relevant to persons in the 21st century.

In Germany today, when a German fills in his income tax form, he has to declare his religion, whether he is a Christian, a Jew, a Muslim, Atheist, etc. Four percent of his taxes then go to the organization representing that belief. After what the Germans have been through under Hitler, for someone to be compelled to record what are his religious beliefs is incredible, to say the least. This tax is a hated tax, as it was in the American States 200 years ago. Moreover, people in Germany do not attend church the way they do in the United States. Since financial support is provided by the State, individuals do not feel that their support is needed, and when people are not involved personally and directly in the support of an institution, they often feel no need to become involved with their time.

In the United States, about $300 billion per year in the form of money, property, stocks, and other goods and services are given by the people to philanthropic organizations. Phenomenal as it may sound, this is practically equivalent to the entire defense budget of the country. A substantial portion of this—as much as 25–28 percent—goes to religious institutions. It was Thomas Jefferson who wrote the Bill for Establishing Religious Freedom, which was finally enacted into law under the guidance of James Madison in 1786. This bill ended the established church in Virginia, and required that support come from church members, not from the state. It had wide influence, and it inspired the First Amendment separation of church and state contained in the U.S. Constitution. There is no question that had it not been for Jefferson's bill for establishing religious freedom and eliminating state support of an established church, the atmosphere in the private sector would never have been created that has encouraged the broad level of individual philanthropy that prevails today. A study of private philanthropy in the United States would find that its real beginning was with this bill by Jefferson that placed responsibility for the support of religious institutions on the individual citizens, and not on the State.

Separation of Church and State

Jefferson had good friends in the clergy, and clergymen were teachers for his grandchildren; but he believed that priests of whatever denomination or religion were capable of great mischief, and surely history demonstrates that he was right. From the age of Constantine to Jefferson's statute for religious freedom—for 1,500 years—tens of millions of people have been tortured, hacked to pieces, and broken on the rack in the name of God. Scholar Arthur Schlesinger once stated, "As a historian, I confess to a certain amusement when I hear the Judeo-Christian tradition praised as a source of our present day concern for human rights." For 1,500 years, what has been carried out against the Jews in the name of God with anti-Semitic slaughter and mayhem by supposed "Christian priests" and "Moslem mullahs" is difficult to believe, yet we know that it did happen. Even in Israel, we have the young man who murdered Prime Minister Rabin. When asked why he did it, his reply was, "God told me to." In our troubled world, we have seen "Moslem human bombs" and "Christian snipers."

The problem created by religion in society is not with God using people, but with people using God. We honor the examples of people like Albert Schweitzer, General George Marshall, and Mother Theresa. We denounce the examples of people like Jim Jones in Guiana, where over 900 died when they administered poison with cups to their children, with spoons to their babies, and then took it themselves. Only three escaped, and again, it was all done in the name of God.

In very simple terms, Jefferson's separation of church and state was designed to prevent people from using God to wreak havoc on their fellow man. What he understood so well, perhaps better than any other statesman of his time and up to the present, is that God can use people and often does, but every time people try to use God, we end up with the Devil. Some present day politicians, even some of those vying for the presidency, have ignored this danger of trying to use God to advance their own purposes, and have attempted to confuse their own purposes with God's purposes in their own minds and certainly in the minds of their constituents. But this is exactly what Jefferson sought to avoid, and what this nation has continued to avoid up unto now, reaping the benefits that derive from this policy. Whether it will be able to continue to do so remains to be seen.

Only eleven years before Jefferson wrote the Bill for Establishing Religious Freedom in Virginia in 1777, a teenager by the name of Chevalier De la Barre was accused in Paris of making rude gestures at a religious procession that went by, of singing rude songs and not taking off his hat, and also of defacing a crucifix. The clergy demanded that his tongue be cut out, his right hand cut off, and that he be burned at the stake. Voltaire tried to come to the aid of the young man in court and finally was able to obtain a concession: the boy was only beheaded.

When Madison sent to Jefferson in Paris the recently enacted Virginia Statute for Establishing Religious Freedom, Jefferson immediately had it translated into French, Italian, and German and distributed throughout Europe. It was received with tremendous acclaim. This document was a breath of fresh air to all but those kings and priests who wished to keep the people under oppression. According to this document written years before by Jefferson, the relationship of a man and a woman to his or her

God was totally their own personal responsibility. Whether a person believed in one God, the Trinity, or no god was their business, not anyone else's. As for the British, they were aghast at all this. They had expected the government of the colonies to disintegrate and self-government to be proved a failure, but the colonies were not falling apart at all! They were not asking the British to come back because they had fallen into a terrible mess fighting each other and were coming apart at the seams. Instead, they were enacting brand new visionary concepts into legislation!

Throughout history, and up to the present time, the world has suffered under wars, massacres, and pogroms perpetrated in the name of God. Religion has been behind the attacks on millions of helpless people in our time, whether it is the Catholics and Protestants of Northern Ireland, the Jews and the Palestinians, the Hindus and Moslems of India, or the numerous other attacks on a smaller scale of various religious minorities in various countries around the globe. And why all this devastation and misery in the name of God? Because peoples the world over are unable to accept the principles set forth by Jefferson in the Declaration of Independence, "that all men are created equal, that they are endowed by their Creator with certain unalienable rights; that among these are life, liberty and the pursuit of happiness." The equal right to worship God or not worship God according to their own consciences in pursuit of their own happiness is denied to minorities both officially by the state, and unofficially by citizens who refuse to live by these principles afforded equally to all citizens.

Foreign Policy That Ignores the Rights of Nations

On September 2, 1945, Ho Chi Minh assembled 500,000 people in Ba Dinh Square in Hanoi, Indochina, later called Vietnam. He had American O.S.S. officers, who had helped him defeat the Japanese in Vietnam, standing on his right-hand side and his famous military strategist, General Giap, standing on his left-hand side. The O.S.S. officers took the salute as the Vietnamese band played the Star Spangled Banner. Then Ho Chi Minh took out of his pocket a copy of Jefferson's Declaration of Independence and started reading: "We hold truths, that all men are created equal, that they are endowed by their Creator with certain unalienable Rights, among these are Life, Liberty and the pursuit of Happiness." He had already set up the Vietnamese-American Friendship Foundation to promote cultural and economical cooperation and development for Indochina. He also appealed to the U.S. Government for diplomatic recognition. He was receptive to just principles, and open to a mutual relationship with the United States. But he was in for the shock of his life. Events would turn him away from the United States and the Western world.

Churchill knew that Roosevelt supported the inalienable rights of the peoples of Asia—the right to self-rule and freedom from the yoke of colonialism—and Churchill understood what this would probably mean for the future of the British Empire. He was able to persuade de Gaulle to demand American support for the return of the French to Indochina; and, thereby he weakened America's resolve for the freedom of peoples under British Colonial rule.

With the death of Roosevelt, so died his idea of an international trusteeship for Indochina after the war. What is often not remembered is that Vichy France had troops in Indochina under the control of the Japanese, and it was a very comfortable arrangement for both parties, though not so for the Vietnamese. It was the French troops that supervised the gathering of the rice crop of 1943 and 1944 and sent it to Tokyo. The estimate was that 1.5 to 2 million Vietnamese died of starvation because of this action. Needless to say, this did not endear the French to the Vietnamese people, and if anything, it increased their resolve to free themselves from colonial rule. The French, on the other hand, were furious at Roosevelt's initial resolve to undermine their colonial position in Indochina.

When Truman became President, he did not know Ho Chi Minh, and felt that he had to honor Roosevelt's promise at Yalta to de Gaulle. Therefore, the United States embarked upon a policy that was directly opposite to its Jeffersonian creed honoring the inalienable right of all peoples to self-determination. We all know the end result of this policy: thirty terrible years that eventually led to American involvement and shook the very foundations of the United States. Both sides to this conflict suffered enormously. The Vietnamese had two million dead and the country practically destroyed. Fifty thousand Americans died, and an enormous economical and social burden followed. From these events came some of the most difficult times for the people of the United States. And all of it resulted from the United States abandoning its Jeffersonian principle of respect for the self-determination of other nations.

Jefferson's Principles

Above all things, this world, this nation, this new generation coming of age needs to know and understand the principles of Jefferson and to demand that their governments embrace those principles and be guided by them in their governing, both at home and abroad. And what are those principles?

As we have seen, the first principle is that all human beings have equal rights to life, liberty, and the pursuit of happiness. All people desire these rights for themselves, but for a free society to exist, they must also desire those rights for every other member of society. Nowhere was this championed more by Jefferson than in the area of religious freedom. In a nation founded on equal rights, the principle must become established that each citizen not only has the right to practice whatever religious belief he has come to adopt, but he has also the right to be free from having the religious beliefs and practices of others imposed upon him under the authority of the government. And beginning with freedom of religion, this same principle of self-government being founded on the equal rights of all citizens is then extended to every area of social interaction, so that all citizens may live in the same nation, under the same flag, but yet enjoy the benefits of those inalienable rights that guarantee each and every one the opportunity to discover the full potential that life holds for them as individuals.

The Chinese historian Prof. Liu Zuochang, who wrote a biography of Jefferson which was published in Beijing in 1990, and who is currently translating Jefferson's writings into Chinese, compares Jefferson with Confucius. He notes that for Jefferson and Confucius, the common man was more important than the state or the church or the leaders. They both believed that the foundation of the spiritual life was the moral life. They both considered family love at the core of human love.

173

They both believed in the primary importance of education. The difference between Jefferson and Confucius was that Confucius set a moral tone and philosophy and practiced it. Jefferson set a moral tone and philosophy, practiced it himself, and at the same time established a political philosophy based on inalienable rights which he believed were the gift of the Creator to mankind, and which he hoped would be recognized eventually around the world. In the words of Abraham Lincoln, "Thomas Jefferson was, is, and perhaps will continue to be, the most distinguished politician of our history." One hundred forty years later, surely that quotation still holds true today, not only for the United States but also for the world. And it appears that many foreigners, having firsthand knowledge of tyranny and oppression, better recognize the importance of Jefferson than do citizens of the United States.

Connor Cruise O'Brien has said that Jefferson cannot be considered a spokesman for human rights because he was a slave-owner. What kind of nonsense is that?! Jefferson inherited property, debt, and slaves. Had he attempted to free his slaves, his creditors would have repossessed them immediately, because they were collateral for his debt. Some of those who embrace the Jefferson-Hemings hoax have suggested that Jefferson was of deficient character, based solely on the fact that he owned slaves. In saying this, however, these people demonstrate that they are completely without any understanding of Mr. Jefferson's dilemma, and are totally ignorant of the many ways he displayed a sterling character in every area of his life. Nowhere was this more evident than in some of the circumstances connected with Jefferson's embroilment in enormous debt, which was also related to his inability to simply release his slaves.

When John Wayles, the father of Jefferson's wife, died in 1773, the Jeffersons inherited his estate, which included Wayles's debts that were owed to the house of Farell & Jones, a British tobacco merchant. These debts, well over a million dollars in today's currency, had been incurred for the purchase of slaves by Wayles, and the slaves served as collateral for the debts. Under the Virginia sequestration law, which was passed during the Revolutionary War, it was possible for these debts to be discharged with depreciated paper currency. Many Virginians of the time, including Patrick Henry, Edmund Pendleton, William Harrison, the Lees, the Marshalls, and many others, all took advantage of this chance to escape their debts. Jefferson, however, refused to take advantage of this opportunity to escape these crushing debts. "Substantial justice is my object, as decided by reason, and not by authority or compulsion," he wrote to his creditor in 1787. Thus we see that the overwhelming burden of debt which Jefferson was to live with for the rest of his life, and which could have been alleviated by his going against his principles, was not a course that Jefferson chose. Few men indeed would have stood so firmly and exercised such strength of character.

Jefferson's ideas about human rights transcend his own circumstances, and indeed transcend time and place. We can determine this, not by arguments based on a misunderstanding of his circumstances and a criticism of his options, but by examining the ideas themselves. In over two hundred years, no one has composed a statement of fundamental human rights that comes anywhere near replacing Jefferson's preamble to the Declaration of Independence.

This, then, is the heritage that Thomas Jefferson has defined for us, and this is what is being threatened along with the attacks on Jefferson's person. In fact, the lies being perpetrated today are much worse than those begun by Callender in 1802. At that time, those lies were told merely to hurt Thomas Jefferson politically, and they were completely ineffectual. Today, the lies are being told not only to hurt Mr. Jefferson, but to denigrate everything he has come to stand for, and ultimately to discredit the foundations upon which this country rests. The stakes are higher today than they have ever been, and we should never hold back from opposing those lies. To treat them as mere differences of scholarly interpretation is to do a disservice to Jefferson, to our nation, and to the truth. Jefferson himself recognized fully the significance of the great principles that he stood for and upon which this nation was founded. Nowhere did he express this more eloquently than in his letter to Roger C. Weightman, mayor of Washington, which Jefferson wrote just ten days before his death. Because of ill health, he declined an invitation to attend a ceremony in 1826 on the 4th of July, the very day on which he was to die. In this letter, he describes his high expectations for the meaning and significance to the whole world of the great principles contained in the Declaration of Independence:

> "May it be to the world, what I believe it will be (to some parts sooner, to others later, but finally to all), the signal of arousing men to burst the chains under which monkish ignorance and superstition had persuaded them to bind themselves, and to assume the blessings and security of self-government. That form which we have substituted, restores the free right to the unbounded exercise of reason and freedom of opinion. All eyes are opened, or opening, to the rights of man. The general spread of the light of science has already laid open to every view the palpable truth that the mass of mankind has not been born with saddles on their backs, nor a favored few booted and spurred, ready to ride them legitimately by the grace of God. These are grounds of hope for others. For ourselves, let the annual return of this day forever refresh our recollection of these rights, and an undiminished devotion to them."

Appendices

Richard E. Dixon

1. Dramatis Personae

2. Madison Hemings Interview

Life Among The Lowly, Madison Hemings, typescript by Rebecca L. McMurry, September 26, 2000, from photocopy of original of March 13, 1874, p. 4, *Pike County (Ohio) Republican.*

3. Last Will of Thomas Jefferson

Will of Thomas Jefferson, typescript by Richard E. Dixon, original in Albemarle County Courthouse, Charlottesville, Virginia, Will Book 8, Page 248.

4. Letter of Ellen Coolidge to Joseph Coolidge

Letter of Ellen Coolidge to her husband Joseph Coolidge, October 24, 1858, typescript by Richard E. Dixon, original in pages 98–102, of the

Ellen Coolidge Letter Book, Coolidge Family Papers, Acc. No. 9090, Special Collections Department, Alderman Library, University of Virginia.

5. Jefferson-Hemings Chronology

Chronology of Jefferson and Hemings Family, prepared by Richard E. Dixon.

Dramatis Personae

James Callender was an editor of the Richmond *Recorder* and wrote a series of articles in 1802 that accused Thomas Jefferson of having a son "Tom" and other children by his slave Sally Hemings. Callender never revealed the sources of his information but his articles indicate he had no personal knowledge of his allegations.

Thomas Jefferson was in his first term as the third president of the United States in 1802 when the articles by Callender were published. No person who had observed his life at Monticello ever wrote or stated that they had observed any expression of intimacy between Jefferson and Sally Hemings from the time she arrived as a small child until Jefferson's death.

Martha Wayles Skelton Jefferson was the daughter of John Wayles and widow of Bathurst Skelton. She married Thomas Jefferson in 1772 and bore him six children, but only two daughters survived to adulthood, Martha (Patsy) and Mary (Polly or Maria). She died of complications from childbirth in 1782.

Martha Jefferson Randolph (Patsy) was only ten years old when she accompanied her father in the lonely rides around Monticello as Jefferson struggled with his grief following the death of Martha Jefferson. This time together forged a lifelong bond of love. She married Thomas Mann Randolph in 1790 and later moved with seven of her children to Monticello. The oldest had recently married and she would have four more.

Ellen Randolph Coolidge was the daughter of Thomas Mann Randolph and Martha Jefferson Randolph. She was born in 1796 and lived most of her life at Monticello until her marriage in 1825 to Joseph Coolidge. It was in 1858 that she wrote the now famous letter which so clearly defines Jefferson's character.

Mary Jefferson Eppes was the second daughter of Thomas and Martha Jefferson to reach adulthood. At the age of nine, she was accompanied on a trans-Atlantic crossing by the young slave girl Sally Hemings, then fourteen, to join Jefferson in Paris. In a sad reminder of her mother's death, she died following complications of childbirth in 1805.

John Wayles was the father of Martha Wayles Jefferson and was accused in an 1805 newspaper article of fathering children by his slave

Betty Hemings, including the child Sally Hemings. Although there is no evidence to support this charge, it has been routinely repeated by historians.

Betty Hemings was the slave of John Wayles and on his death was inherited by Martha Jefferson. Her large family became household servants and artisans at Monticello. Jefferson seemed to favor the Hemings, granting manumission to two of Betty's sons and later freeing one son and four of her grandsons in his will.

Sally Hemings was born in 1773 to Betty Hemings and came to Monticello as a part of the inheritance of John Wayles to his daughter Martha Jefferson. She bore four children who reached adulthood, Beverly, Harriet, Madison, and Eston. They were probably legally white under Virginia law, although their fathers are not known. During her lifetime, including the eight years after she left Monticello as a "free" woman, she never claimed Jefferson fathered her children.

Beverly Hemings was the oldest adult child of Sally Hemings, born in 1798, and listed in Jefferson's farm book as a "runaway" in 1822. He was believed to be legally white, but his father is unknown.

Harriet Hemings was born in 1801 and said to be "white as anybody," although her father is not known. She is also listed in Jefferson's farm book as a "runaway" in 1822, although Jefferson's overseer said she left with Jefferson's assistance.

Madison Hemings was born in 1805 and is believed to have been legally white, although his father is not known. He was freed by Jefferson's will in 1827 and eventually migrated to Ohio. He gave an interview in 1873 which is the "document" relied on for the claim that his mother, Sally Hemings, became Jefferson's concubine in Paris and that Jefferson fathered her four adult children.

Eston Hemings was born in 1808 and is believed to have been legally white. His father is not known, but may have been one of eight Jeffersons living in the vicinity of Monticello, including Thomas Jefferson, since one of his descendants was shown by the recent DNA testing to possess the Y chromosome haplotype common to the Jefferson males. It is speculated he was the "one case" mentioned by Thomas Jefferson Randolph in an 1858 interview, of a "resemblance" to Jefferson.

Dramatis Personae

Thomas Jefferson Randolph was the eldest son of Martha Jefferson Randolph and became the executor of his grandfather's will. He was the subject of an interview sometime in 1858 by Jefferson biographer Henry Randall, in which Randolph denied that Thomas Jefferson was the father of Sally Hemings' children.

Edmund Bacon was on overseer at Monticello for the period 1806–1815. In an interview in 1862, he stated that he did not believe Jefferson was the father of Harriet Hemings, and recalled some other male coming from Sally Hemings' room "many a morning."

James Hemings was a son of Betty Hemings and accompanied Jefferson to Paris in 1783. He was there when his sister Sally arrived in 1787. He was freed by Jefferson in 1796 but never claimed that Jefferson fathered any of Sally Hemings' children.

Robert Hemings was a son of Betty Hemings and a brother of Sally Hemings. He traveled frequently as a free man and was set free by Jefferson in 1794. Robert could read and write but never claimed any paternity by Jefferson of Sally Hemings' children.

Madison Hemings Interview

Typescript by Rebecca L. McMurry, made September 26, 2000, from a photocopy of the original article, "Life Among the Lowly, No. 1" from the March 13, 1873, issue of the *Pike County (Ohio) Republican*, p. 4. Two passages in the fourth paragraph of the photocopy used for this typescript were indistinct, and the words supplied by Fawn Brodie (*Thomas Jefferson: An Intimate History*, New York, 1974) were used. These two passages are in bold face.

Editor's Note: Words underlined in the text below and followed by a superscript reference number were changed in the version of this Interview that appeared in the book, *Thomas Jefferson and Sally Hemings: An American Controversy*, by Annette Gordon-Reed. Please refer to the notes at the end of the Interview for an explanation. We fail to understand why the TJMF, in conducting what was supposed to be a "comprehensive review," used this altered version of the interview rather than making a transcription from the original.

******

I never knew of but one white man who bore the name of Hemings; he was an Englishman and my greatgrandfather. He was captain of an English trading vessel which sailed between England and Williamsburg, Va., then quite a port.

My grandmother[1] was a fullblooded African, and possibly a native of that country. She was the property of John Wales, a Welchman. Capt. Hemings happened to be in the port of Williamsburg at the time my grandmother was born, and acknowledging her fatherhood he tried to purchase her of Mr. Wales, who would not part with the child, though he was offered an extraordinarily large price for her. She was named Elizabeth Hemings. Being thwarted in the purchase, and determining to own his flesh[2] and blood he resolved to take the child by force or stealth, but the knowledge of his intention coming to John Wales' ears, through leaky fellow servants of the mother, she and the child were taken into the "great house" under their master's immediate care. I have been informed that it was not the extra value of that child over other slave children that induced Mr. Wales to refuse to sell it, for slave masters then, as in later days, had no compunctions of conscience which restrained them from parting mother and child of however tender age, but he was restrained by the fact that just about that time amalgamation began, and the child was so great a curiosity that its owner desired to raise it himself that he might see its outcome. Capt. Hemings soon afterwards sailed from Williamsburg, never to return. Such is the story that comes down to me.

Elizabeth Hemings grew to womanhood in the family of John Wales, whose wife dying she (Elizabeth) was taken by the widower Wales as his concubine, by whom she had six children—three sons and three daughters, viz: Robert, James, Peter, Critty, Sally and Thena. These children went by the name of Hemings.

Williamsburg was the capital of Virginia, and of course it was an aristocratic place, where the "bloods" of the Colony and the new **State most did** congregate. Thomas Jefferson, the author of the Declaration of Independence, was educated at William and Mary College, which had its seat at Williamsburg. He afterwards studied law with Geo. Wythe, and practiced law at the bar of the general court of the Colony. He was afterwards elected a member of the provincial legislature from Albemarle County. Thos. Jefferson was a visitor at the "great house" of John Wales, who had children about his own age. He formed the acquaintance of his daughter Martha (I believe that was her name, though I am not positively sure,) and an intimacy sprang up between them which ripened into love, and they were married. They afterwards went to live at his country seat, Monticello, and in course of time had born to them a daughter whom they named Martha. About the time she was born my mother, the second daughter of John Wales and Elizabeth Hemings was born. On the death of John Wales, my grandmother, his concubine, and her children by him fell to Martha, Thomas Jefferson's wife, and consequently became the property of Thomas Jefferson, who in the **course of time became** famous, and was appointed minister to France during our revolutionary troubles, or soon after independence was gained. About the time of the appointment and before he was ready to leave the country his wife died, and as soon after her interment as he could attend to and arrange his domestic affairs in accordance with the changed circumstances of his family in consequence of this misfortune (I think not more than three weeks there-

183

after) he left for France, taking his eldest daughter with him. He had had sons born to him, but they died in early infancy, so he then had but two children—Martha and Maria. The latter was left at home, but was afterwards ordered to follow him to France. She was three years or so younger than Martha. My mother accompanied her as her body servant. When Mr. Jefferson went to France <u>Martha was a young woman grown, my mother was about her age and Maria was just budding into womanhood.</u>[3] Their stay (my mother and Maria's) was about eighteen months. But during that time my mother became Mr. Jefferson's concubine, and when he was called back home she was *enceinte* by him. He desired to bring my mother back to Virginia with him but she demurred. She was just beginning to understand the French language well, and in France she was free, while if she returned to Virginia she would be re-enslaved. So she refused to return with him. To induce her to do so he promised her extraordinary privileges, and made a solemn pledge that her children should be freed at the age of twenty-one years. In consequence of his promises, on which she implicitly relied, she returned with him to Virginia. Soon after their arrival, she gave birth to a child, of whom Thomas Jefferson was the father. It lived but a short time. She gave birth to four others, and Jefferson was the father of all of them. Their names were Beverly, Harriet, Madison (myself), and Eston—three sons and one daughter. We all became free agreeably to the treaty entered into by our parents before we were born. We all married and have raised families.

Beverly left Monticello and went to Washington as a white man. He married a white woman in Maryland, and their only child, a daughter, was not known by the white folks to have any colored blood coursing in her veins. Beverly's wife's family were people in good circumstances.

Harriet married a white man in good standing in Washington City, whose name I could give, but will not, for prudential reasons. She raised a family of children, and so far as I know they were never suspected of being tainted with African blood in the community where she lived or lives. I have not heard from her for ten years, and do not know whether she is dead or alive. She thought it to her interest, on going to Washington, to assume the role of a white woman, and by her dress and conduct as such I am not aware that her identity as Harriet Hemings of Monticello has ever been discovered.

Eston married a colored woman in Virginia, and moved from there to Ohio, and lived in Chillicothe several years. In the fall of 1852 he removed to Wisconsin, where he died a year or two afterwards. He left three children.

As to myself, I was named Madison by the wife of James Madison, who was afterwards President of the United States. Mrs. Madison happened to be at Monticello at the time of my birth, and begged the privilege of naming me, promising my mother a fine present for the honor. She consented, and Mrs. Madison dubbed me by the name I now acknowledge, but like many promises of white folks to the slaves she never gave my mother anything. I was born at my father's seat of Monticello, in Albemarle county, Va., near Charlottesville, on the 19th day of January, 1805. My very earliest recollections are of my grandmother Elizabeth Hemings. That was when I was about three years old. She was sick and upon her death bed. I was eating a piece of bread and asked her if she would have some. She replied: "No; granny don't want bread any more." She shortly afterwards breathed her last. I have only a faint recollection of her.

Of my father, Thomas Jefferson, I knew more of his domestic than his public life, during his life time. It is only since his death that I have learned much of the latter, except that he was considered as a foremost man in the land, and held many important trusts, including that of President. I learned to read by inducing the white children to teach me the letters and something more; what else I know of books I have picked up here and there, till now I can read and write. I was almost 21 1/2 years of age when my father died, on the 4th of July, 1826.

About his own home he was the quietest of men. He was hardly ever known to get angry, though sometimes he was irritated when matters went wrong, but even then he hardly ever allowed himself to be made unhappy any great length of time. Unlike Washington he had but little taste or care for agricultural pursuits. He left matters pertaining to his plantations mostly with his stewards and overseers. He always had mechanics at work for him, such as carpenters, blacksmiths, shoemakers, coopers, etc. It was his mechanics he seemed mostly to direct, and in their operations he took great interest. Almost every day of his latter years he might have been seen among them. He occupied much of the time in his office engaged in correspondence and reading and writing. His general temperament was smooth and even; he was very undemonstrative. He was uniformly kind to all about him. He was not in the habit of showing partiality or fatherly affection to us children. We were the only children of his by a slave woman. He was affectionate toward his white grandchildren, of whom he had fourteen, twelve of whom lived to manhood and womanhood. His daughter Martha married Thomas Mann Randolph by whom she had thirteen children. Two died in infancy. The names of the living were Ann, Thomas Jefferson, Ellen, Cornelia, Virginia, Mary, James, Benj. Franklin, Lewis Madison, Septimia and Geo. Wythe. Thos. Jefferson Randolph was Chairman of the Democratic National Convention in Baltimore last spring which nominated Horace Greeley for the Presidency, and Geo. Wythe Randolph was Jeff. Davis' first Secretary of War in the late "unpleasantness."

Maria married John Epps, and raised one son—Francis.

My father generally enjoyed excellent health. I never knew him to have but one spell of sickness, and that was caused by a visit to the Warm Springs in 1818. Till within three weeks of his death he was hale and hearty, and at the age of 83 years he walked erect and with stately tread. I am now 68, and I well remember that he was a much smarter man physically, even at that age, than I am.

When I was fourteen years old I was put to the carpenter trade under the charge of John Hemings, the youngest son of my grandmother. His father's name was Nelson, who was an Englishman. She had seven children by white men and seven by colored men—fourteen in all. My brothers, sister Harriet and myself, were used alike. <u>They were put to some mechanical trade at the age of fourteen. Till then</u>[4] we were permitted to stay about the "great house," <u>and required</u>[5] to do such light work as going on errands. Harriet learned to spin and to weave in a little factory on the home plantation. We were free from the dread of having to be slaves all our lives long, and were measurably happy. We were always permitted to be with our mother, who was well used. It was her duty, all her life which I can remember, up to the time of father's death, to take care of his chamber and wardrobe, look after us children and do such light work as sewing, &c. Provision was made in the will of our father that we should be freed when we arrived at the age of 21 years. We had all passed that period when he died but Eston, and he was given the remainder of his time shortly after. He and I rented a house and took mother to live with us, till her death, which event occurred in 1835.

In 1831[6] I married Mary McCoy. Her grandmother was a slave, and lived with her master, Stephen Hughes, near Charlottesville, as his wife. She was manumitted by him, which made their children free born. Mary McCoy's mother was his daughter. I was about 23 and she 23[7] years of age when we married. We lived and labored together in Virginia till 1836, when we voluntarily left and came to Ohio. We settled in Pebble township, Pike county. We lived there four or five years, and during my stay in the county I worked at my trade on and off for about four years. Joseph Sewell was my first employer. I built for him what is now known as Bizzleport[8] No. 2, in Waverly. I afterwards worked for George Wolfe, Senior, and did the carpenter work of the brick building now owned by John J. Kellison, in which the Pike County Republican is printed. I worked for and with Micajah[9] Hinson. I found him to be a very clever man. I also reconstructed the building on the corner of Market and Water streets from a store to a hotel for the late Judge Jacob Row.

When we came from Virginia we brought one daughter (Sarah) with us, leaving the dust of a son in the soil near Monticello. We have had born to us in this State nine children. Two are dead. The names of the living, besides Sarah, are Harriet, Mary Ann, Catharine, Jane, William Beverly, James Madison and Ellen Wales. Thomas Eston died in the Andersonville prison pen, and Julia died at home. William, James and Ellen are unmarried and live at home, in Huntington township, Ross county. All the others are married and raising families. My post-office address is Pee Pee, Pike county, Ohio.

Portions of Text Altered

The underlined passages in the above text were altered in the version of this Interview that appeared in the book, *Thomas Jefferson and Sally Hemings: An American Controversy,* by Annette Gordon-Reed. The numbers below refer to the passages noted in the text.

1. "grandmother" was changed to "great grandmother"

2. "determining to own his flesh" was changed to "determined to own his own flesh"

3. "Martha was a young woman grown, my mother was about her age and Maria was just budding into womanhood." was changed to "Martha was just budding into womanhood."

4. "They were put to some mechanical trade at the age of fourteen. Till then" was omitted completely.

5. "and required" was changed to "and only required"

6. "1831" was changed to "1834"

7. "about 23 and she 23" was changed to "about 28 and she 22"

8. "Bizzleport" was changed to "Rizzleport"

9. "Micajah" was changed to "Micajab"

Last Will of Thomas Jefferson

I Thomas Jefferson of Monticello in Albemarle being of sound mind and in my ordinary state of health make my last will and testament in manner & form as follows:

I give to my grandson Francis Epps son of my dear deceased daughter Mary Epps in fee simple all that part of my lands at poplar Forest lying west of the following lines to wit. Beginning at Radford's upper corner near the double branches of Bear Creek and the public road & running thence in a straight line to the fork of my private road near the barn thence along that private road (as it was changed in 1817) to its crossing of the main branch of north Tomahawk Creek and from that crossing in a direct line over the main ridge which divided the North & South Tomahawk to South Tomahawk at the confluence of two branches where the old road to the waterlick crossed it and from that confluence up the northernmost branch which seperates McDaniel & Perrys Field to its source & thence by the shortest line to my western boundary. And having in a former correspondence with my deceased son in law John W. Eps contemplated laying off for him with remainder to my grand son Francis a certain portion in the southern part of my lands in Bedford and Campbell which I afterwards found to be generally more indifferent than I had supposed and therefore determined to change its location for the better now to remove all doubt if any could arise on a purpose merely voluntary and unexecuted I hereby declare that what I have herein given to my sd. grandson Francis is instead of and not additional to what I had formerly contemplated.

I subject all my other property to the payment of my debts in the first place, considering the insolvent state of the affairs of my friend & son in law Thomas Mann Randolph, and that what will remain of my property will be the only resource against the want in which his family would otherwise be left it must be his wish as it is my duty to guard that resource against all liability for his debts engagements or purposes whatsoever and to preclude the rights powers and authorities over it which might result to him by operation of law and which might independently of his will bring it within the power of his creditors I do hereby desire and bequeath all the residue of my property real and personal in possession or in action whether held in my own right or in that of my dear deceased wife according to the powers vested in me by deed of settlement for the purpose to my grandson Thomas J. Randolph & my friends Nicholas P. Trist and Alex Garret & their heirs

      Th. Jefferson

    during the life of my son in law Thomas M. Randolph to be held to and administered by them in trust for the sole and separate use and behoof of my dear daughter Martha Randolph and heirs and aware of the nice and difficult distinctions of the law in these cases I will further explain by saying that I understand and intend the effect of these limitation to be that legal estate and actual occupation shall be vested in my said trustees and held by them in base fee determinable on the death of my said son in law and the remainder during the same time be vested in my said daughter and her heirs and of course disposable by her last will and that at the death of my sd. so in law the particular estate of the sd. trustees shall be determined and the remainder in legal estate possession and use become vested in my sd. daughter and her heirs in absolute property forever. In consequence of the varrity and indescribableness of the articles of property within the house at Monticello, and the difficulty of inventorying and appraising them separately and specifically and its inutility I dispense with having them inventoried and appraised and it is my will that my Executors be not hold to give any security for the administration of my Estate. I appoint my grand son Thomas Jefferson Randolph my sole executor during his life and after his death I constitute executors my Friends Nicholas P. Trist and Alexander Garrett joining to them my daughter Martha Randolph after the death of my sd son in law Thomas M Randolph.- Lastly I revoke all former wills by me hereby made and in witness that this is my will I have written the whole with my own hand on two pages and have subscribed my name to each of them this 16th day of March one thousand eight hundred and twenty six.

      Th Jefferson

    I Thomas Jefferson of Monticello in Albemarle made and add the following codicil to my will controlling the same so far as its provisions go

Last Will

I recommend to my daughter Martha Randolph the maintenance and care of my well beloved sister Ann Scott Marks and trust confidently that from affection to her as well as for my sake she will never let her want a comfort.- I have made no specifick provisions for the comfortable maintenance of my son in law Thomas M. Randolph because of the difficulty and uncertainty of devising terms which shall vest any beneficial interest in him which the law will not transfer to the benefit of his creditors to the destitution of my daughter and her family and disablement of her to supply him whereas property placed under the executive right of my daughter and her independent will as if she were a feme sole considering the relations in which she both to him and his children will be a certain resource against want for all. I give to my friend James Madison of montpelier my gold mounted walking staff of animal horn as a token of the cordial and affectionate friendship which for nearly now an half century, has united us in the same principles and pursuits of what we have deemed for the greatest good of our country. I give to the university of Virginia my library except such particular books only and of the same edition as it may already possess when this legacy shall take effect the rest of my said library remaining after those given to the university shall have been taken out I give to my two grandsons in law Nicholas P. Trist and Joseph Coolidge.

To my grandson Thomas Jefferson Randolph I give my silver watch in preference of the golden one because of its superior excellence. my papers of business going of course to him as my executor all others of a literary or other caracter I give him as of his own property.

Th. Jefferson

I give a gold watch to each of my grand children who shall not have already received one from me to be purchased and delivered by executors to my grand sons at the of 21 and grand daughters at that of sixteen.

I give to my good affectionate and faithful servant Burwell his freedom and the sum of three hundred Dollars to buy necessaries to commence his trade of painter and glaser, or to use otherwise as he pleases. I give also to my good servants John Hemings and Joe Fosset their freedom at the end of one year after my death and to each of them respectively all the tools of their respective shops or callings and it is my will that a comfortable log house be built for each of the three servants so emancipated on some part of my lands convenient to them with respect to the residence of their wives and to Charlottesville and the university where they be mostly employed and reasonably convenient also to the interest of the proprietor of the land: of which houses I give the use of one with a heritage of an acre to each during his life or personal occupation thereof — I give also to John Hemings the service of his two apprentices Madison and Eston Hemings until their respective ages of twenty one years at which period respectively I give them their freedom and I Humbly and earnestly request of the legislature of Virginia a confirmation of the bequest of freedom to these servants with permission to remain in this state where their families and connections are as an additional instance of favor of which I have received so many other manifestations in the course of my life and for which I now give them my last solemn thanks.

In testimony that this is a codicil to my will of yesterdays date and that it is to modify so far the provision of that will I have written it all with my own hand in two pages, to each of which I subscribe my name this 17th day of march one thousand eight hundred and twenty six
Th Jefferson

A court held for Albemarle county the 7th of August 1826.

This Instrument of writing purporting to be the last will and testament of Thomas Jefferson Deceased was produced into court and the hand writing of the testator proved by the oath of Valentine W Southall and ordered to be recorded.
Teste
Alexander Garrett CC

Typescript by Richard E. Dixon
Will of Thomas Jefferson
Recorded Albemarle County Land Records
Will Book 8, Page 248

Letter of Ellen Coolidge
to Joseph Coolidge

Letter of Ellen Coolidge to her husband Joseph Coolidge, October 24, 1858, original in pages 98–102, of the Ellen Coolidge Letter Book, Coolidge Family Papers, Acc. No. 9090, Special Collections Department, Alderman Library, University of Virginia. Typescript by Richard E. Dixon.

Editor's Note: Words underlined in the text below and followed by a superscript reference number were changed in the version of this letter that appeared in the book, *Thomas Jefferson and Sally Hemings: An American Controversy*, by Annette Gordon-Reed. Please refer to the notes at the end of the letter for an explanation of the changes. Changes in punctuation made by Gordon-Reed were not noted. Words underlined in the original document were rendered in italics here. We fail to understand why the TJMF, in conducting what was supposed to be a "comprehensive review," used this altered version of the letter rather than making a transcription from the original. We note especially that the sentence "No female domestic ever entered his chambers except at hours when he was known not to be there and none could have entered without being exposed to the public gaze" was changed in the Gordon-Reed version to "No female domestic ever entered his chambers except at hours when he was known not to be in the public gaze."

*****

To Joseph Coolidge _____ Copy
Edgehill. 24. October 1858

I am just from church, a church originally planned by grandpapa, where I heard a good sermon from an Episcopalian Clergyman, a young man, the Revd. Mr. Butler.

I have been talking freely with my brother Jefferson on the subject of the "yellow children" and will give you the substance of our conversation, with my subsequent reflections.

It is difficult to prove a negative. It is impossible to prove that Mr. Jefferson never had a coloured mistress or coloured children and that these children were never sold as slaves. The latter part of the charge however is disproved by it's atrocity, and it's utter disagreement with the general character and conduct of Mr. Jefferson, acknowledged to be a humane man and eminently a kind master. Would he who was always most considerate of the feelings and the well being of his slaves, treat them barbarously only when they happened to be his own children, and leave them to be sold in a distant market when he might have left them free—as you know he did several of his slaves, directing his executor to petition the Legislature of Virginia for leave for them to remain in the state after they were free—Some of them are here to this day.

It was his principle (I knew that of my own knowledge) to allow such of his slaves as were sufficiently white to pass for white men, to withdraw quietly from the plantation; it was called running away, but they were never reclaimed. I remember four instances of this, three young men and one girl, who walked away and staid away—Their whereabouts was perfectly known but they were left to themselves—for they were white enough to pass for white. Some of the children currently reported to be Mr. Jefferson's were about the age of his own grandchildren. Of course he must have been carrying on his intrigues in the midst of his daughters family and insulting the sanctity of home by his prolificacy. But he had a large family of grandchildren of all ages, older & younger. Young men and young girls. He lived whenever he was at Monticello, and entirely for the last seventeen years of his life, in the midst of these young people, surrounded by them—his intercourse with them of the freest and most affectionate kind. How comes it that his immoralities were never suspected by his own family—that his daughter and her children rejected with horror and contempt the charges brought against him? That my brother, then a young man certain to know all that was going on behind the scenes, positively declares his indignant <u>disbelief</u>[1] in the imputations and solemnly affirms that he never saw or heard the smallest thing which could lead him to suspect that his grandfather's life was other than perfectly pure. His apartment had no private entrance not perfectly accessible and visible to all the household. No female domestic ever entered his chambers except at hours when he was known not to be there and none could have entered without being exposed to[2] the public gaze. But again I would put it to any fair mind to decide if a man so admirable in his domestic character as Mr. Jefferson so devoted to his daughters and their children, so fond of their society, so tender, considerate, refined in his intercourse with them, so watchful over them in all respects, would be likely to rear a race of half-breeds under their eyes and carry on his low amours in the circle of his family.

Now many causes existed which might have given rise to suspicions, setting aside the inveterate rage and malice of Mr. Jefferson's traducers.

The house at Monticello was a long time in building and was principally built by Irish workmen. These men were known to have had children of whom the mothers were black women. But these women were much better pleased to have it supposed that such children were their master's. "Le Czar m'a fait l'honneur de me faire cet enfant." There were dissipated young men in the neighborhood who sought the society of the mulatresses and they in like manner were not anxious to establish any claim of paternity in the results of such associations. One woman known to Mr. J. Q. Adams and others as "dusky Sally" was pretty notoriously the mistress of a married man, a near relation of Mr. Jefferson's, and there can be small question that her children were his. They were all fair and all set free at my grandfather's death, or had been suffered to absent themselves permanently before he died. The mother, Sally Hemings, had accompanied Mr. Jefferson's younger daughter to Paris and was lady's maid to both sisters. Again I ask is it likely that so fond so anxious a father, whose letters to his daughters are replete with tenderness and with good counsels for their conduct, should (when there were so many other objects upon whom to fix his elicit attentions) have selected the female attendant of his own pure children to become his paramour! The thing will not bear telling. There are such things, after all[3], as moral impossibilities.

The habit that the southern slaves have of adopting their masters names is another cause of misrepresentation and misapprehension. There is no doubt that such of Mr. Jefferson's slaves as were sold after his death would call themselves by his name. One very notorious villain who never had been the property of Mr. Jefferson, took his name and proclaimed himself his son. He was as black as a crow, and born during Mr. Jefferson's absence abroad, or under some other circumstances which rendered the truth of his assertion simply impossible.

I have written thus far thinking you might chuse to communicate my letter to Mr. Bulfinch. Now I will tell you in confidence what Jefferson told me under the like condition. Mr. Southall and himself being[4] young men together, heard Mr. Peter Carr say with a laugh, that "the old gentleman had to bear the blame of his and Sam's (Col. Carr) misdeeds."

There is a general impression that the four children of Sally Hemings were *all* the children of Col. Carr, the most notorious good natured Turk that ever was master of a black seraglio kept at other men's expense. His deeds are as well known as his name.— I have written in very[5] great haste for I have very little time to write We sat down sixteen at my brother's table to-day, and are never less than twelve—Children, grand-children, visitors, friends—I am in a perfect whirl—yet this is the way in which I lived during all my girlish days, and then it seemed the easi-est and most natural thing imaginable—Now I wonder how my head can bear it long. But Jefferson and Jane are the most affectionate parents and the kindest neighbors that I know.

Portions of Text Altered

The underlined passages in the above text were altered in the version of this Interview that appeared in the book, *Thomas Jefferson and Sally Hemings: An American Controversy,* by Annette Gordon-Reed. The num-bers below refer to the passages noted in the text.

1. "disbelief" was changed to "belief"
2. "there and none could have entered without being exposed to" was omitted and replaced with "in"
3. "all" was omitted entirely
4. "being" was omitted entirely
5. "very" was omitted entirely

Jefferson-Hemings Chronology

THOMAS JEFFERSON	TIMELINE	HEMINGS FAMILY
Birth of Thomas Jefferson	13 Apr 1743	
Jefferson enters William & Mary	1760	
Jefferson graduates, studies law with George Wythe	1762	
Jefferson passes bar exam	1765	
Construction begins on Monticello	1768	
Shadwell burns down	1770	
Jefferson marries Martha Wayles Skelton	1 Jan 1772	
Martha Jefferson (Patsy) born	17 Sep 1772	
Death of John Wayles	28 May 1773	Martha Jefferson inherits Hemings family
	1773	Birth of Sally Hemings
Jane Randolph Jefferson born	3 Apr 1774	
Jane Randolph Jefferson dies	1 Sep 1775	
	1775	Betty Hemings and children come to Monticello
Declaration of Independence	4 Jul 1776	
Son Jefferson born	28 May 1777	
Son Jefferson dies	14 Jun 1777	
Mary Jefferson (Polly and Maria) born	1 Aug 1778	
Lucy Elizabeth Jefferson born	30 Nov 1778	
Jefferson elected governor of Virginia	1779–1780	
Lucy Elizabeth Jefferson dies	15 Apr 1781	
Lucy Elizabeth Jefferson (II) born	8 May 1782	
Death of Jefferson's wife, Martha Jefferson	6 Sep 1782	

Thomas Jefferson	Timeline	Hemings Family
Jefferson goes to Paris with daughter Martha (Patsy)	Jul 1784	James Hemings accompanies Jefferson to Paris
Lucy Elizabeth Jefferson (II) dies	13 Oct 1784	
Daughter Mary joins Jefferson in Paris	Jul 1787	Sally Hemings accompanies Mary to Paris
Jefferson returns to Monticello	Dec 1789	Sally and James return with Jefferson
Martha (Patsy) marries Thomas Mann Randolph, Jr.	23 Feb 1790	
Jefferson becomes Secretary of State	1790	
	1790	Birth of Tom Woodson to Sally (?)
Jefferson resigns as Secretary of State	1793	
	5 Oct 1795	Birth of Harriet I to Sally
Jefferson elected vice-president	1796	
Mary (Polly) marries John Wayles Eppes	13 Oct 1797	
	Dec 1797	Death of Harriet I
	1 Apr 1798	Birth of Beverly Hemings to Sally
	7 Dec 1799	Birth/death of daughter to Sally (?)
Jefferson elected President	1800	
	May 1802	Birth of Harriet Hemings II to Sally
	Sep–Oct 1802	Callender articles in Richmond *Recorder*
Death of Mary Jefferson	17 Apr 1804	
Jefferson reelected President	1804	
	19 Jan 1805	Birth of Madison Hemings to Sally

Jefferson-Hemings Chronology

Thomas Jefferson	Timeline	Hemings Family
	21 May 1808	Birth of Eston Hemings to Sally
Jefferson retires to Monticello	March 1809	
Founding of the University of Virginia	1817	
Jefferson land values drop in Panic of 1819	1819	
	1822	Harriet and Beverly "run away"
University of Virginia opens its doors	1825	
Death of Thomas Jefferson	4 Jul 1826	
	1827	Madison and Eston freed by Jefferson's will
	1827	Sally Hemings leaves with Madison and Eston
	1835	Death of Sally Hemings

Contributors and Reviewers

The opinions and views expressed in this book are those of the contributors, and are not to be interpreted as representing those of the Scholars Commission for the Study of the Jefferson-Hemings Controversy, which is a completely independent and separate group of scholars doing its own research and publication.

Although each article in this book was the principal responsibility of the person named as author, many of the ideas developed herein were the result of a team effort, with all the members of The Thomas Jefferson Heritage Society making contributions to the development of the various lines of inquiry through email exchanges. Often, one person would express the kernel of a particular idea, another would develop it further, a third would reapply it in a particular conceptual framework, and a fourth would then incorporate it into one of the articles for this book. None of us claim these insights and ideas as an exclusive property; we are all grateful to our fellow-members for assistance received and given. For these reasons, we list all the board members of The Thomas Jefferson Heritage Society, because, whether responsible for an article or only for reviewing and commenting on articles written by others, all contributed in important ways towards the creation of this book.

President
John H. Works, Jr., lineal descendant of Thomas Jefferson, Monticello Association member, and former Monticello Association president. Mr. Works is President & Chief Executive Officer of Rompetrol, 222 Calea Victoriei, 71104 Bucharest, Romania. His phone number is: (011) 4094-3-777-22 and his email address is: JohnHWorks@aol.com.

Vice President
Bahman Batmanghelidj, builder, long-time student of Thomas Jefferson, and a member of the Jefferson Legacy Foundation. His phone numbers are: office, 703-406-1800, cell phone, 703-963-1945.

Secretary
Pamela Buell, collateral descendant of Thomas Jefferson and Jefferson-Hemings research assistant.

Treasurer
C. Michael Moffitt, Ph.D., Jefferson researcher and former Monticello guide. Dr. Moffitt is a former executive in the environmental consulting and analytical laboratory field.

Jefferson Family Researcher
Herbert Barger is founder of the TJHS, Jefferson researcher, and assisted Dr. Eugene Foster in identifying subjects for DNA comparisons and provided family charts and history. Mr. Barger lives in Ft. Washington, Maryland. His phone number is 301-292-2739, his email address is herbar@erols.com, and his webpage is www.angelfire.com/va/TJTruth.

Publications Director
Eyler Robert Coates, Sr., is editor-compiler of the Jefferson Quotations website at UVA (etext.virginia.edu/jefferson/quotations) and several other Jefferson-related websites. Mr. Coates is former head librarian at Shenandoah University, and formerly a supervisor at the Library of Congress. He lives in Louisiana, his phone number is 504-885-7959, and his email address is publdir@eyler.freeservers.com.

Legal Counsel
Richard E. Dixon, Attorney at Law, Jefferson researcher, and author of evidentiary study on Jefferson paternity issues. Mr. Dixon is a graduate of Duke University and the University of Virginia Law School. He has practiced law for 40 years in Fairfax, Virginia, where he still maintains a law office. He can be reached at 4122 Leonard Drive, Fairfax, VA 22030,

phone number 703-691-0770, fax number 703-691-0978, and email address redixonlaw@aol.com.

Funding and Development Director
Sharon Liko, Patriot and Jefferson researcher.

Jefferson-Hemings Inquiry Coordinator
White M. Wallenborn, M.D., Jefferson researcher, former Monticello guide, author of the TJMF Minority Report on the Jefferson-Hemings DNA Study.

Associate
Frank B. Buell, Jr., Patriot and Jefferson-Hemings research assistant.

Associate
James F. McMurry, Jr., M.D., has many years experience in family genealogy and researching early Virginia history. He and Mrs. McMurry published their book, *Jefferson, Callender and the Sally Story*, in September, 2000.

Associate
Rebecca McMurry is a family genealogist and has combined that with an interest in early Virginia history. Her ancestors lived in Albemarle and adjacent counties, not too far from Monticello.

Guest Contributor
David Murray, Ph.D., Director, Statistical Assessment Service (STATS), a non-partisan, non-profit research organization in Washington, D.C. STATS is devoted to the accurate use of scientific and social research in public policy debate. It is the preeminent organization for statistical analysis in the nation's capitol and in the United States. Their website is located at www.stats.org/.

Index

Index

The Last Word

Public relations for The Thomas Jefferson Heritage Society are being handled by the following firm:

LH3, Inc.—Interactive Marketing Agency
2525 15th St. Suite #18
Denver, CO 80211
Phone 720-855-6443
Contact: donna@lh3.com
Website: www.LH3.com

For the latest information on the Jefferson-Hemings controversy and on The Scholars Commission for the Study of the Jefferson-Hemings Controversy, visit the website of The Thomas Jefferson Heritage Society at:

http://www.tjheritage.org

Contributions to the society are cheerfully accepted, and may be sent to the following address:

C. Michael Moffitt, Treasurer
The Thomas Jefferson Heritage Society
P. O. Box 4482
Charlottesville, VA 22905-4482